THE
WOMEN'S
TOPICAL BIBLE

KING JAMES VERSION

PNEUMALIFE PUBLISHING

Pneuma Life Publishing books are available at discounted prices for bulk purchase for fund-raising, premiums, sales promotions.

For details, email your request to **sales@pneumalife.com** or write us at **Pneuma Life Publishing, 12138 Central Ave, Suite 251, Mitchellville, MD 20721**

THE WOMEN'S TOPICAL BIBLE
Published by Pneuma Life Publishing
12138 Central Ave, Suite 251,
Mitchellville, MD 20721
www.pneumalife.com

JUNE 2025

All rights reserved. No part of this publication may be reproduced, distributed, or transmitted in any form or by any means, including photocopying, recording, or other electronic or mechanical methods, without the prior written permission of the publisher, except in the case of brief quotations embodied in critical reviews and certain other non-commercial uses permitted by copyright law. For permission requests, write to the publisher, addressed "Attention: Permissions Coordinator," at the address below.

Unless otherwise noted, all Sciptures quotations are from the KJV of the Bible

Copyright © 2025 by D. Stewart
All Rights Reserved
Printed in the United States of America
ISBN 978-1-56229-872-2

Table of Contents
THE WOMEN'S TOPICAL BIBLE
SECTION I: IDENTITY & CALLING

Woman as God's Daughter	2
Created in God's Image	3
Woman's Divine Purpose	4
God's Love for Women	6
Woman's Worth and Value	7
Fearfully and Wonderfully Made	8
Woman's Spiritual Gifts	9
Called and Chosen	10
Woman's Unique Design	12
Beloved of God	13
Woman's Spiritual Authority	14
Divine Feminine Strengths	15
God's Plan for Women	16
Woman's Eternal Perspective	17
Daughters of the King	18
Woman's Spiritual Identity	19
God's Promises to Women	20
Woman's Kingdom Purpose	21
Chosen Generation	22
Royal Priesthood (Women)	24

Woman's Calling in Christ	25
Vessels of Honor	26
Woman's Spiritual Inheritance	27
God's Masterpiece	28
Woman as Light Bearer	29
Woman's Destiny	30
God's Favor on Women	31
Woman's Divine Potential	32
Blessed Among Women	33
Woman's Sacred Mission	34

SECTION II: CHARACTER & VIRTUE

The Proverbs 31 Woman	36
Godly Character	37
Woman of Excellence	38
Virtuous Woman	39
Noble Character	40
Inner Beauty	41
Gentle and Quiet Spirit	42
Woman of Integrity	43
Wisdom in Women	44
Discerning Woman	45

Woman of Faith	46
Courageous Woman	47
Strong Woman	48
Compassionate Heart	49
Gracious Woman	50
Patient Woman	51
Humble Heart	52
Self-Control for Women	53
Contentment in Women	54
Thankful Heart	55
Pure Heart	56
Merciful Woman	57
Peacemaking Woman	58
Righteous Woman	59
Holy Living for Women	60

SECTION III: RELATIONSHIPS

Marriage and Wives	62
Single Woman's Life	63
Sisterhood and Friendship	64
Mother-Daughter Relationships	65
Mentoring Women	66

Community of Women	67
Submission in Marriage	68
Helpmeet and Partnership	69
Conflict Resolution	70
Forgiveness in Relationships	71
Love and Romance	72
Preparing for Marriage	73
Supporting Other Women	74
Encouraging Others	75
Building Bridges	76
Hospitality	77
Serving Together	78
Unity Among Women	79
Godly Communication	79
Loyalty and Faithfulness	80
Boundaries in Relationships	81
Dealing with Difficult People	82
Women's Ministry	83
Discipleship of Women	84
Accountability Partners	85

SECTION IV: MOTHERHOOD & PARENTING

Motherhood	88
Pregnancy and Childbirth	89
Raising Godly Children	90
Training Children	91
Mother's Love	92
Discipline and Correction	93
Teaching Children God's Word	94
Praying for Children	95
Single Motherhood	96
Stepparenting	97
Grandmotherhood	98
Childlessness and Infertility	99
Adoption	100
Protective Mother	100
Nurturing Children	101
Mother's Wisdom	102
Sacrificial Love (Mothers)	103
Working Mothers	104
Homeschooling Mothers	105
Empty Nest Mothers	106

SECTION V: SPIRITUAL GROWTH

Woman's Prayer Life	108
Studying God's Word	109
Worship and Praise	110
Fasting for Women	111
Spiritual Disciplines	112
Growing in Faith	113
Overcoming Doubt	114
Trusting God	115
Surrendering to God	116
Walking in the Spirit	117
Fruit of the Spirit	118
Spiritual Warfare for Women	119
Intercession and Prayer	120
Hearing God's Voice	121
Obedience to God	122
Seeking God's Will	123
Spiritual Maturity	124
Testimony and Witness	125
Evangelism for Women	126
Ministry and Service	127

SECTION VI: EMOTIONAL & MENTAL HEALTH

Overcoming Depression	130
Dealing with Anxiety	131
Managing Stress	132
Healing from Trauma	133
Self-Image and Confidence	134
Overcoming Fear	135
Finding Peace	136
Joy in Trials	137
Hope in Difficult Times	138
Emotional Healing	139
Mental Strength	140
Overcoming Negative Thoughts	141
Building Resilience	142
Comfort in Grief	143
Renewed Mind	144

SECTION VII: PRACTICAL LIVING

Time Management	146
Work and Career	147

Financial Stewardship	148
Health and Wellness	149
Home Management	150
Decision Making	151
Leadership for Women	152
Speaking and Communication	153
Setting Priorities	154
Goal Setting	155
Organization and Planning	156
Creativity and Talents	157
Education and Learning	158
Technology and Modern Life	159
Balance in Life	160

SECTION VIII: CHALLENGES & TRIALS

Overcoming Adversity	162
Dealing with Rejection	163
Facing Criticism	164
Betrayal and Hurt	165
Loneliness	166
Disappointment	167

Failure and Setback	168
Persecution for Faith	169
Health Challenges	170
Financial Difficulties	171
Family Conflicts	172
Workplace Challenges	173
Aging Gracefully	174
Loss and Grief	175
Transition and Change	176

SECTION IX: BIBLICAL WOMEN EXAMPLES

Women of Faith (Old Testament)	178
Women of Faith (New Testament)	179
Courageous Women of the Bible	180
Wise Women of Scripture	181
Mothers in the Bible	182
Leaders Among Biblical Women	183
Worshipping Women	184
Serving Women	185
Faithful Women	186
Transformed Women	187

SECTION X:
SPECIAL SEASONS & PURPOSE

Seasons of Waiting	190
Times of Celebration	191
Woman's Ministry Calling	192
Legacy and Inheritance	193
Eternal Perspective for Women	194

INTRODUCTION

You Were Born for Such a Time as This.

There comes a moment in every woman's life when she stands at the intersection of her circumstances and her calling, wondering if God truly sees her struggles, hears her prayers, and has a purpose for her pain. You may be in that place right now—feeling overlooked, overwhelmed, or uncertain about your next steps. Let me tell you something that will shift your perspective forever: God didn't create you to merely survive your circumstances; He designed you to transform them.

The Women's Topical Bible was born from a profound understanding that women face unique challenges, carry distinct burdens, and possess extraordinary potential that often goes untapped. While the Bible speaks to all humanity, there are specific truths, promises, and principles that address the female heart, mind, and experience in ways that can revolutionize your life.

This isn't just another study tool sitting on your shelf—this is your personal arsenal of divine weapons crafted specifically for the battles you face as a woman. Whether you're navigating the complexities of marriage, raising children who seem bent on testing every boundary, climbing corporate ladders while maintaining your integrity, or simply trying to discover who you really are beneath all the roles you play, God's Word has something powerful to say to you.

Within these pages, you'll discover 180 carefully curated topics that speak directly to your heart's deepestconcerns and highest aspirations. From understanding your identity as God's daughter to walking in theauthority He's given you, from building meaningful relationships to overcoming the fears that have heldyou back, every topic is designed to move you from where you are to where God intends you to be.

The women of Scripture weren't perfect—they were powerful. Sarah laughed at God's promises butbecame the mother of nations. Rahab's past was questionable, but her faith was unshakeable. Esther feltinadequate for her assignment, but she saved an entire people. Mary was young and inexperienced, butshe carried the Savior of the world. What made them extraordinary wasn't their perfection; it was theirwillingness to trust God's word over their circumstances.
You carry that same potential. You possess that same power. You serve that same God.

Every scripture compilation in this book has been selected to address the real issues you face—from theboardroom to the bedroom, from the nursery to the empty nest, from seasons of abundance to momentsof absolute desperation. This is practical theology for practical women who need practical answers for animpractical world.

As you journey through these pages, prepare for transformation. Prepare for breakthrough. Prepare tosee yourself not as the world has labeled you, but as God has destined you. Your finest hour isn't behindyou—it's ahead of you. Your greatest victory isn't in your past—it's in your future. Your most powerfultestimony isn't what you've overcome—it's what you're about to conquer. Turn the page. Yourbreakthrough begins now.

SECTION I:
IDENTITY
&
CALLING

Woman as God's Daughter

But as many as received him, to them gave he power to become the sons of God, even to them that believe on his name. John 1:12

For ye are all the children of God by faith in Christ Jesus. For as many of you as have been baptized into Christ have put on Christ. There is neither Jew nor Greek, there is neither bond nor free, there is neither male nor female: for ye are all one in Christ Jesus. Galatians 3:26-28

And will be a Father unto you, and ye shall be my sons and daughters, saith the Lord Almighty. 2 Corinthians 6:18

Behold, what manner of love the Father hath bestowed upon us, that we should be called the sons of God: therefore the world knoweth us not, because it knew him not. Beloved, now are we the sons of God, and it doth not yet appear what we shall be: but we know that, when he shall appear, we shall be like him; for we shall see him as he is. 1 John 3:1-2

Having predestinated us unto the adoption of children by Jesus Christ to himself, according to the good pleasure of his will. Ephesians 1:5

For as many as are led by the Spirit of God, they are the sons of God. For ye have not received the spirit of bondage again to fear; but ye have received the Spirit of adoption, whereby we cry, Abba, Father. The Spirit itself beareth witness with our spirit, that we are the children of God: And if children, then heirs; heirs of God, and joint-heirs with Christ; if so be that we suffer with him, that we may be also glorified together. Romans 8:14-17

But when the fulness of the time was come, God sent forth his Son, made of a woman, made under the law, To redeem them that were under the law, that we might receive the adoption of sons. And because ye are sons, God hath sent forth the Spirit of his Son into your hearts, crying, Abba, Father.

Whereforethou art no more a servant, but a son; and if a son, then an heir of God through Christ. Galatians 4:4-7

Like as a father pitieth his children, so the Lord pitieth them that fear him. Psalms 103:13

If ye then, being evil, know how to give good gifts unto your children, how much more shall your Fatherwhich is in heaven give good things to them that ask him? Matthew 7:11

A woman's true identity is not found in her roles or achievements, but in her relationship with Godas His beloved daughter. - Beth Moore

Created in God's Image

And God said, Let us make man in our image, after our likeness: and let them have dominion over the fishof the sea, and over the fowl of the air, and over the cattle, and over all the earth, and over every creeping thing that creepeth upon the earth. So God created man in his own image, in the image of God createdhe him; male and female created he them. Genesis 1:26-27

This is the book of the generations of Adam. In the day that God created man, in the likeness of Godmade he him; Male and female created he them; and blessed them, and called their name Adam, in theday when they were created. Genesis 5:1-2

And the Lord God formed man of the dust of the ground, and breathed into his nostrils the breath of life;and man became a living soul. Genesis 2:7

And the Lord God said, It is not good that the man should be alone; I will make him an help meet for him.Genesis 2:18

And the Lord God caused a deep sleep to fall upon Adam, and he slept: and he took one of his ribs, andclosed up the flesh instead thereof; And the rib, which the Lord God had taken from man, made he awoman, and brought her unto the man. And Adam said, This is now bone of my bones, and flesh of myflesh: she shall be called Woman, because she was taken out of Man. Genesis 2:21-23

For a man indeed ought not to cover his head, forasmuch as he is the image and glory of God: but thewoman is the glory of the man.
1 Corinthians 11:7

Whoso sheddeth man's blood, by man shall his blood be shed: for in the image of God made he man.Genesis 9:6

For he knew his works from the beginning of the world. Acts 15:18

Woman was created as the crown of creation, bearing the image of God with divine purpose andeternal significance.

Woman's Divine Purpose

For I know the thoughts that I think toward you, saith the Lord, thoughts of peace, and not of evil, to giveyou an expected end. Jeremiah 29:11

For we are his workmanship, created in Christ Jesus unto good works, which God hath before ordainedthat we should walk in them. Ephesians 2:10

And we know that all things work together for good to them that love God, to them who are the calledaccording to his purpose. For whom he did foreknow, he also did predestinate to be conformed to theimage of his Son, that he might be the firstborn among many brethren. Moreover whom he didpredestinate, them he also called: and whom he called, them he also justified: and whom he justified,them he also glorified. Romans 8:28-30

According as he hath chosen us in him before the foundation of the world, that we should be holy andwithout blame before him in love: Having predestinated us unto the adoption of children by Jesus Christto himself, according to the good pleasure of his will.
Ephesians 1:4-5

Who hath saved us, and called us with an holy calling, not according to our works, but according to hisown purpose and grace, which was given us in Christ Jesus before the world began. 2 Timothy 1:9

But ye are a chosen generation, a royal priesthood, an holy nation, a peculiar people; that ye should shewforth the praises of him who hath called you out of darkness into his marvellous light. 1 Peter 2:9

The Lord will perfect that which concerneth me: thy mercy, O Lord, endureth for ever: forsake not theworks of thine own hands.
Psalms 138:8

Being confident of this very thing, that he which hath begun a good work in you will perform it until theday of Jesus Christ.
Philippians 1:6

For it is God which worketh in you both to will and to do of his good pleasure. Philippians 2:13

In whom also we have obtained an inheritance, being predestinated according to the purpose of himwho worketh all things after the counsel of his own will. Ephesians 1:11

God's purpose for each woman is unique and irreplaceable—discover yours and walk boldly in it. -Priscilla Shirer

God's Love for Women

For God so loved the world, that he gave his only begotten Son, that whosoever believeth in him shouldnot perish, but have everlasting life. John 3:16

The Lord hath appeared of old unto me, saying, Yea, I have loved thee with an everlasting love: thereforewith lovingkindness have I drawn thee. Jeremiah 31:3

But God commendeth his love toward us, in that, while we were yet sinners, Christ died for us. Romans 5:8

Herein is love, not that we loved God, but that he loved us, and sent his Son to be the propitiation for oursins. 1 John 4:10

And we have known and believed the love that God hath to us. God is love; and he that dwelleth in lovedwelleth in God, and God in him. 1 John 4:16

We love him, because he first loved us. 1 John 4:19

For the Father himself loveth you, because ye have loved me, and have believed that I came out fromGod. John 16:27

He that loveth me shall be loved of my Father, and I will love him, and will manifest myself to him. John14:21

As the Father hath loved me, so have I loved you: continue ye in my love. John 15:9

Can a woman forget her sucking child, that she should not have compassion on the son of her womb?yea, they may forget, yet will I not forget thee. Behold, I have graven thee upon the palms of my hands;thy walls are continually before me. Isaiah 49:15-16

Like as a father pitieth his children, so the Lord pitieth them that fear him. Psalms 103:13

The Lord thy God in the midst of thee is mighty; he will save, he will rejoice over thee with joy; he will restin his love, he will joy over thee with singing. Zephaniah 3:17

God's love for you as a woman is not based on your performance but on His unchanging characterand choice to love you eternally.

Woman's Worth and Value

Are not two sparrows sold for a farthing? and one of them shall not fall on the ground without yourFather. But the very hairs of your head are all numbered. Fear ye not therefore, ye are of more value thanmany sparrows. Matthew 10:29-31

Consider the ravens: for they neither sow nor reap; which neither have storehouse nor barn; and Godfeedeth them: how much more are ye better than the fowls? Luke 12:24

But even the very hairs of your head are all numbered. Fear not therefore: ye are of more value thanmany sparrows. Luke 12:7

What is man, that thou art mindful of him? and the son of man, that thou visitest him? For thou hastmade him a little lower than the angels, and hast crowned him with glory and honour. Psalms 8:4-5

For ye are bought with a price: therefore glorify God in your body, and in your spirit, which are God's. 1Corinthians 6:20

Forasmuch as ye know that ye were not redeemed with corruptible things, as silver and gold, from yourvain conversation received by tradition from your fathers; But with the precious blood of Christ, as of alamb without blemish and without spot. 1 Peter 1:18-19

Since thou wast precious in my sight, thou hast been honourable, and I have loved thee: therefore will Igive men for thee, and people for thy life. Isaiah 43:4

Whose adorning let it not be that outward adorning of plaiting the hair, and of wearing of gold, or ofputting on of apparel; But let it be the hidden man of the heart, in that which is not corruptible, even the ornament of a meek and quiet spirit, which is in the sight of God of great price. 1 Peter 3:3-4

She is more precious than rubies: and all the things thou canst desire are not to be compared unto her.Proverbs 3:15

A woman's value is not determined by the world's standards but by God's eternal love and theprice He paid for her soul.

Fearfully and Wonderfully Made

I will praise thee; for I am fearfully and wonderfully made: marvellous are thy works; and that my soulknoweth right well. My substance was not hid from thee, when I was made in secret, and curiouslywrought in the lowest parts of the earth. Thine eyes did see my substance, yet being unperfect; and in thybook all my members were written, which in continuance were fashioned, when as yet there was none ofthem. How precious also are thy thoughts unto me, O God! how great is the sum of them! Psalms 139:14-17

For thou hast possessed my reins: thou hast covered me in my mother's womb. Psalms 139:13

Before I formed thee in the belly I knew thee; and before thou camest forth out of the womb I sanctifiedthee, and I ordained thee a prophet unto the nations. Jeremiah 1:5

Thus saith the Lord that made thee, and formed thee from the womb, which will help thee; Fear not, OJacob, my servant; and thou, Jesurun, whom I have chosen. Isaiah 44:2

Did not he that made me in the womb make him? and did not one fashion us in the womb? Job 31:15

Know ye that the Lord he is God: it is he that hath made us, and not we ourselves; we are his people, and the sheep of his pasture. Psalms 100:3

But now, O Lord, thou art our father; we are the clay, and thou our potter; and we all are the work of thy hand. Isaiah 64:8

The Spirit of God hath made me, and the breath of the Almighty hath given me life. Job 33:4

And the Lord God formed man of the dust of the ground, and breathed into his nostrils the breath of life; and man became a living soul. Genesis 2:7

You are not an accident or a mistake—you are God's intentional masterpiece, crafted with divine purpose.

Woman's Spiritual Gifts

Now there are diversities of gifts, but the same Spirit. And there are differences of administrations, but the same Lord. And there are diversities of operations, but it is the same God which worketh all in all. But the manifestation of the Spirit is given to every man to profit withal. 1 Corinthians 12:4-7

As every man hath received the gift, even so minister the same one to another, as good stewards of the manifold grace of God.
1 Peter 4:10

For to one is given by the Spirit the word of wisdom; to another the word of knowledge by the same Spirit; To another faith by the same Spirit; to another the gifts of healing by the same Spirit; To another the working of miracles; to another prophecy; to another discerning of spirits; to another divers kinds of tongues; to another the interpretation of tongues:

But all these worketh that one and the selfsame Spirit, dividing to every man severally as he will. 1 Corinthians 12:8-11

Having then gifts differing according to the grace that is given to us, whether prophecy, let us prophesy according to the proportion of faith; Or ministry, let us wait on our ministering: or he that teacheth, on teaching; Or he that exhorteth, on exhortation: he that giveth, let him do it with simplicity; he that ruleth, with diligence; he that sheweth mercy, with cheerfulness. Romans 12:6-8

Wherefore I put thee in remembrance that thou stir up the gift of God, which is in thee by the putting on of my hands. 2 Timothy 1:6
Neglect not the gift that is in thee, which was given thee by prophecy, with the laying on of the hands of the presbytery.
1 Timothy 4:14

And it shall come to pass in the last days, saith God, I will pour out of my Spirit upon all flesh: and your sons and your daughters shall prophesy, and your young men shall see visions, and your old men shall dream dreams: And on my servants and on my handmaidens I will pour out in those days of my Spirit; and they shall prophesy.
Acts 2:17-18

For the gifts and calling of God are without repentance.
Romans 11:29

God has uniquely gifted every woman for His purposes—discover your gifts and use them for His glory.

Called and Chosen

But ye are a chosen generation, a royal priesthood, an holy nation, a peculiar people; that ye should shew forth the praises of him who hath called you out of darkness into his marvellous light. 1 Peter 2:9

According as he hath chosen us in him before the foundation of the world, that we should be holy andwithout blame before him in love. Ephesians 1:4

Ye have not chosen me, but I have chosen you, and ordained you, that ye should go and bring forth fruit,and that your fruit should remain: that whatsoever ye shall ask of the Father in my name, he may give ityou. John 15:16

Who hath saved us, and called us with an holy calling, not according to our works, but according to hisown purpose and grace, which was given us in Christ Jesus before the world began. 2 Timothy 1:9

And we know that all things work together for good to them that love God, to them who are the calledaccording to his purpose. Romans 8:28

Moreover whom he did predestinate, them he also called: and whom he called, them he also justified:and whom he justified, them he also glorified. Romans 8:30

But God hath chosen the foolish things of the world to confound the wise; and God hath chosen theweak things of the world to confound the things which are mighty; And base things of the world, andthings which are despised, hath God chosen, yea, and things which are not, to bring to nought things thatare. 1 Corinthians 1:27-28

For many are called, but few are chosen. Matthew 22:14

Wherefore the rather, brethren, give diligence to make your calling and election sure: for if ye do thesethings, ye shall never fall. 2 Peter 1:10

Your calling is not a burden to bear but a privilege to embrace—you are chosen for such a time asthis. - Esther 4:14

Woman's Unique Design

And the Lord God said, It is not good that the man should be alone; I will make him an help meet for him. Genesis 2:18

And the rib, which the Lord God had taken from man, made he a woman, and brought her unto the man. And Adam said, This is now bone of my bones, and flesh of my flesh: she shall be called Woman, becauseshe was taken out of Man. Genesis 2:22-23

For the man is not of the woman; but the woman of the man. Neither was the man created for thewoman; but the woman for the man. Nevertheless neither is the man without the woman, neither thewoman without the man, in the Lord. For as the woman is of the man, even so is the man also by thewoman; but all things of God.
1 Corinthians 11:8-12

The aged women likewise, that they be in behaviour as becometh holiness, not false accusers, not givento much wine, teachers of good things; That they may teach the young women to be sober, to love theirhusbands, to love their children, To be discreet, chaste, keepers at home, good, obedient to their ownhusbands, that the word of God be not blasphemed. Titus 2:3-5

Who can find a virtuous woman? for her price is far above rubies. The heart of her husband doth safelytrust in her, so that he shall have no need of spoil. She will do him good and not evil all the days of her life. Proverbs 31:10-12

Strength and honour are her clothing; and she shall rejoice in time to come. She openeth her mouth withwisdom; and in her tongue is the law of kindness. Proverbs 31:25-26

Her children arise up, and call her blessed; her husband also, and he praiseth her. Proverbs 31:28

God designed women with unique strengths, intuition, and capabilities that complement andcomplete His divine plan.

Beloved of God

The Lord thy God in the midst of thee is mighty; he will save, he will rejoice over thee with joy; he will restin his love, he will joy over thee with singing. Zephaniah 3:17

Yea, I have loved thee with an everlasting love: therefore with lovingkindness have I drawn thee. Jeremiah31:3

But God, who is rich in mercy, for his great love wherewith he loved us, Even when we were dead in sins,hath quickened us together with Christ, (by grace ye are saved;) And hath raised us up together, andmade us sit together in heavenly places in Christ Jesus: That in the ages to come he might shew theexceeding riches of his grace in his kindness toward us through Christ Jesus. Ephesians 2:4-7

And we have known and believed the love that God hath to us. God is love; and he that dwelleth in lovedwelleth in God, and God in him. 1 John 4:16

Herein is love, not that we loved God, but that he loved us, and sent his Son to be the propitiation for oursins. 1 John 4:10

We love him, because he first loved us. 1 John 4:19

Behold, what manner of love the Father hath bestowed upon us, that we should be called the sons ofGod: therefore the world knoweth us not, because it knew him not. 1 John 3:1

As the Father hath loved me, so have I loved you: continue ye in my love. John 15:9

I in them, and thou in me, that they may be made perfect in one; and that the world may know that thouhast sent me, and hast loved them, as thou hast loved me. John 17:23

You are deeply loved by God—not because of what you do, but because of who you are to Him.

Woman's Spiritual Authority

And Jesus came and spake unto them, saying, All power is given unto me in heaven and in earth. Go yetherefore, and teach all nations, baptizing them in the name of the Father, and of the Son, and of the Holy Ghost: Teaching them to observe all things whatsoever I have commanded you: and, lo, I am with youalway, even unto the end of the world. Amen. Matthew 28:18-20

Behold, I give unto you power to tread on serpents and scorpions, and over all the power of the enemy:and nothing shall by any means hurt you. Luke 10:19

And these signs shall follow them that believe; In my name shall they cast out devils; they shall speak withnew tongues; They shall take up serpents; and if they drink any deadly thing, it shall not hurt them; theyshall lay hands on the sick, and they shall recover.
Mark 16:17-18

But ye shall receive power, after that the Holy Ghost is come upon you: and ye shall be witnesses unto meboth in Jerusalem, and in all Judaea, and in Samaria, and unto the uttermost part of the earth. Acts 1:8

And it shall come to pass in the last days, saith God, I will pour out of my Spirit upon all flesh: and yoursons and your daughters shall prophesy, and your young men shall see visions, and your old men shalldream dreams: And on my servants and on my handmaidens I will pour out in those days of my Spirit;and they shall prophesy.
Acts 2:17-18

Submit yourselves therefore to God. Resist the devil, and he will flee from you. James 4:7

For we wrestle not against flesh and blood, but against principalities, against powers, against the rulers ofthe darkness of this world, against spiritual wickedness in high places. Ephesians 6:12

Finally, my brethren, be strong in the Lord, and in the power of his might. Put on the whole armour of God, that ye may be able to stand against the wiles of the devil. Ephesians 6:10-11

And whatsoever ye shall ask in my name, that will I do, that the Father may be glorified in the Son. If ye shall ask any thing in my name, I will do it. John 14:13-14

Greater is he that is in you, than he that is in the world. 1 John 4:4

Women possess the same spiritual authority as men through Christ—step boldly into your God-given power and purpose.

Divine Feminine Strengths

Strength and honour are her clothing; and she shall rejoice in time to come. She openeth her mouth with wisdom; and in her tongue is the law of kindness. Proverbs 31:25-26

A gracious woman retaineth honour: and strong men retain riches. Proverbs 11:16

Every wise woman buildeth her house: but the foolish plucketh it down with her hands. Proverbs 14:1

She girdeth her loins with strength, and strengtheneth her arms. Proverbs 31:17

The heart of her husband doth safely trust in her, so that he shall have no need of spoil. She will do him good and not evil all the days of her life. Proverbs 31:11-12

She looketh well to the ways of her household, and eateth not the bread of idleness. Her children arise up, and call her blessed; her husband also, and he praiseth her. Proverbs 31:27-28

And above all these things put on charity, which is the bond of perfectness. Colossians 3:14

But the fruit of the Spirit is love, joy, peace, longsuffering, gentleness, goodness, faith, Meekness,temperance: against such there is no law. Galatians 5:22-23

She stretcheth out her hand to the poor; yea, she reacheth forth her hands to the needy. Proverbs 31:20

Divine feminine strengths are gifts from God—use them to bless others and build His kingdom.

God's Plan for Women

For I know the thoughts that I think toward you, saith the Lord, thoughts of peace, and not of evil, to giveyou an expected end. Jeremiah 29:11

And we know that all things work together for good to them that love God, to them who are the calledaccording to his purpose.
Romans 8:28

For we are his workmanship, created in Christ Jesus unto good works, which God hath before ordainedthat we should walk in them. Ephesians 2:10

Being confident of this very thing, that he which hath begun a good work in you will perform it until theday of Jesus Christ.
Philippians 1:6

But ye are a chosen generation, a royal priesthood, an holy nation, a peculiar people; that ye should shewforth the praises of him who hath called you out of darkness into his marvellous light. 1 Peter 2:9

The steps of a good man are ordered by the Lord: and he delighteth in his way. Psalms 37:23

Trust in the Lord with all thine heart; and lean not unto thine own understanding. In all thy waysacknowledge him, and he shall direct thy paths. Proverbs 3:5-6

Many are the plans in a man's heart, but it is the Lord's purpose that prevails. Proverbs 19:21

In whom also we have obtained an inheritance, being predestinated according to the purpose of himwho worketh all things after the counsel of his own will. Ephesians 1:11

God's plan for your life is perfect—trust His timing and His ways even when you can't see the fullpicture.

Woman's Eternal Perspective

While we look not at the things which are seen, but at the things which are not seen: for the things whichare seen are temporal; but the things which are not seen are eternal. 2 Corinthians 4:18

For our light affliction, which is but for a moment, worketh for us a far more exceeding and eternal weightof glory. 2 Corinthians 4:17

Set your affection on things above, not on things on the earth. For ye are dead, and your life is hid withChrist in God. When Christ, who is our life, shall appear, then shall ye also appear with him in glory. Colossians 3:2-4

And this is the promise that he hath promised us, even eternal life. 1 John 2:25

For God so loved the world, that he gave his only begotten Son, that whosoever believeth in him shouldnot perish, but have everlasting life. John 3:16

And this is life eternal, that they might know thee the only true God, and Jesus Christ, whom thou hastsent. John 17:3

But lay up for yourselves treasures in heaven, where neither moth nor rust doth corrupt, and where thieves do not break through nor steal. For where your treasure is, there will your heart be also. Matthew 6:20-21

For we know that if our earthly house of this tabernacle were dissolved, we have a building of God, an house not made with hands, eternal in the heavens. 2 Corinthians 5:1

And God shall wipe away all tears from their eyes; and there shall be no more death, neither sorrow, nor crying, neither shall there be any more pain: for the former things are passed away. Revelation 21:4

Live with eternity in mind—your temporal struggles are preparing you for an eternal weight of glory.

Daughters of the King

But as many as received him, to them gave he power to become the sons of God, even to them that believe on his name. John 1:12

And will be a Father unto you, and ye shall be my sons and daughters, saith the Lord Almighty. 2 Corinthians 6:18

But ye are a chosen generation, a royal priesthood, an holy nation, a peculiar people; that ye should shew forth the praises of him who hath called you out of darkness into his marvellous light. 1 Peter 2:9

Behold, what manner of love the Father hath bestowed upon us, that we should be called the sons of God: therefore the world knoweth us not, because it knew him not. 1 John 3:1

The Spirit itself beareth witness with our spirit, that we are the children of God: And if children, then heirs; heirs of God, and joint-heirs with Christ; if so be that we suffer with him, that we may be also glorified together. Romans 8:16-17

For ye are all the children of God by faith in Christ Jesus.
Galatians 3:26

And because ye are sons, God hath sent forth the Spirit of his Son into your hearts, crying, Abba, Father.Wherefore thou art no more a servant, but a son; and if a son, then an heir of God through Christ.
Galatians 4:6-7

In whom also we have obtained an inheritance, being predestinated according to the purpose of himwho worketh all things after the counsel of his own will. Ephesians 1:11

The king's daughter is all glorious within: her clothing is of wrought gold. Psalms 45:13

You are not just anyone—you are a daughter of the King of Kings, with royal blood flowingthrough your veins.

Woman's Spiritual Identity

Therefore if any man be in Christ, he is a new creature: old things are passed away; behold, all things arebecome new. 2 Corinthians 5:17

I am crucified with Christ: nevertheless I live; yet not I, but Christ liveth in me: and the life which I now livein the flesh I live by the faith of the Son of God, who loved me, and gave himself for me.
Galatians 2:20

For ye are dead, and your life is hid with Christ in God. When Christ, who is our life, shall appear, thenshall ye also appear with him in glory.
Colossians 3:3-4

But ye are a chosen generation, a royal priesthood, an holy nation, a peculiar people; that ye should shewforth the praises of him who hath called you out of darkness into his marvellous light. 1 Peter 2:9

And you, being dead in your sins and the uncircumcision of your flesh, hath he quickened together withhim, having forgiven you all trespasses. Colossians 2:13

For by grace are ye saved through faith; and that not of yourselves: it is the gift of God: Not of works, lestany man should boast. Ephesians 2:8-9

Know ye not that ye are the temple of God, and that the Spirit of God dwelleth in you? 1 Corinthians 3:16

Wherefore come out from among them, and be ye separate, saith the Lord, and touch not the uncleanthing; and I will receive you.
2 Corinthians 6:17

For we are his workmanship, created in Christ Jesus unto good works, which God hath before ordainedthat we should walk in them. Ephesians 2:10

Your identity is not found in your roles, relationships, or achievements—it is found in Christ alone.- Jennifer Rothschild

God's Promises to Women

For all the promises of God in him are yea, and in him Amen, unto the glory of God by us. 2 Corinthians1:20

Heaven and earth shall pass away, but my words shall not pass away. Matthew 24:35

God is not a man, that he should lie; neither the son of man, that he should repent: hath he said, and shallhe not do it? or hath he spoken, and shall he not make it good? Numbers 23:19

Whereby are given unto us exceeding great and precious promises: that by these ye might be partakersof the divine nature, having escaped the corruption that is in the world through lust. 2 Peter 1:4

Being confident of this very thing, that he which hath begun a good work in you will perform it until theday of Jesus Christ.
Philippians 1:6

And my God shall supply all your need according to his riches in glory by Christ Jesus. Philippians 4:19

Come unto me, all ye that labour and are heavy laden, and I will give you rest. Take my yoke upon you,and learn of me; for I am meek and lowly in heart: and ye shall find rest unto your souls. For my yoke iseasy, and my burden is light. Matthew 11:28-30

Call unto me, and I will answer thee, and shew thee great and mighty things, which thou knowest not.Jeremiah 33:3

The Lord thy God in the midst of thee is mighty; he will save, he will rejoice over thee with joy; he will restin his love, he will joy over thee with singing. Zephaniah 3:17

God's promises are your inheritance as His daughter—claim them with confidence andexpectation.

Woman's Kingdom Purpose

But seek ye first the kingdom of God, and his righteousness; and all these things shall be added unto you.Matthew 6:33

But ye are a chosen generation, a royal priesthood, an holy nation, a peculiar people; that ye should shewforth the praises of him who hath called you out of darkness into his marvellous light. 1 Peter 2:9

And Jesus came and spake unto them, saying, All power is given unto me in heaven and in earth. Go yetherefore, and teach all nations, baptizing them in the name of the Father, and of the Son, and of the HolyGhost: Teaching them to observe all things whatsoever I have commanded you: and, lo, I am with youalway, even unto the end of the world. Amen. Matthew 28:18-20

For we are his workmanship, created in Christ Jesus unto good works, which God hath before ordainedthat we should walk in them. Ephesians 2:10

Ye are the light of the world. A city that is set on an hill cannot be hid. Neither do men light a candle, andput it under a bushel, but on a candlestick; and it giveth light unto all that are in the house. Let your lightso shine before men, that they may see your good works, and glorify your Father which is in heaven.Matthew 5:14-16

And he said unto them, Go ye into all the world, and preach the gospel to every creature. Mark 16:15

As we have therefore opportunity, let us do good unto all men, especially unto them who are of thehousehold of faith. Galatians 6:10

Pure religion and undefiled before God and the Father is this, To visit the fatherless and widows in theiraffliction, and to keep himself unspotted from the world. James 1:27

Your kingdom purpose as a woman is to advance God's kingdom through your unique gifts,calling, and sphere of influence.

Chosen Generation

But ye are a chosen generation, a royal priesthood, an holy nation, a peculiar people; that ye should shewforth the praises of him who hath called you out of darkness into his marvellous light. 1 Peter 2:9

According as he hath chosen us in him before the foundation of the world, that we should be holy andwithout blame before him in love. Ephesians 1:4

Ye have not chosen me, but I have chosen you, and ordained you, that ye should go and bring forth fruit,and that your fruit should remain:

that whatsoever ye shall ask of the Father in my name, he may give ityou. John 15:16

But God hath chosen the foolish things of the world to confound the wise; and God hath chosen theweak things of the world to confound the things which are mighty; And base things of the world, andthings which are despised, hath God chosen, yea, and things which are not, to bring to nought things thatare: That no flesh should glory in his presence. 1 Corinthians 1:27-29

For many are called, but few are chosen. Matthew 22:14

But we are bound to give thanks alway to God for you, brethren beloved of the Lord, because God hathfrom the beginning chosen you to salvation through sanctification of the Spirit and belief of the truth. 2Thessalonians 2:13

Elect according to the foreknowledge of God the Father, through sanctification of the Spirit, untoobedience and sprinkling of the blood of Jesus Christ: Grace unto you, and peace, be multiplied. 1 Peter1:2

Who hath saved us, and called us with an holy calling, not according to our works, but according to hisown purpose and grace, which was given us in Christ Jesus before the world began. 2 Timothy 1:9

You are part of a chosen generation, specifically selected by God for such a time as this.

Royal Priesthood (Women)

But ye are a chosen generation, a royal priesthood, an holy nation, a peculiar people; that ye should shewforth the praises of him who hath called you out of darkness into his marvellous light. 1 Peter 2:9

And hath made us kings and priests unto God and his Father; to him be glory and dominion for ever andever. Amen. Revelation 1:6

And hast made us unto our God kings and priests: and we shall reign on the earth. Revelation 5:10

But the hour cometh, and now is, when the true worshippers shall worship the Father in spirit and in truth:for the Father seeketh such to worship him. God is a Spirit: and they that worship him must worship himin spirit and in truth. John 4:23-24

I beseech you therefore, brethren, by the mercies of God, that ye present your bodies a living sacrifice,holy, acceptable unto God, which is your reasonable service. Romans 12:1

Ye also, as lively stones, are built up a spiritual house, an holy priesthood, to offer up spiritual sacrifices,acceptable to God by Jesus Christ. 1 Peter 2:5

By him therefore let us offer the sacrifice of praise to God continually, that is, the fruit of our lips givingthanks to his name. Hebrews 13:15

And it shall come to pass in the last days, saith God, I will pour out of my Spirit upon all flesh: and yoursons and your daughters shall prophesy, and your young men shall see visions, and your old men shalldream dreams: And on my servants and on my handmaidens I will pour out in those days of my Spirit;and they shall prophesy. Acts 2:17-18

As a woman in the royal priesthood, you have direct access to God and the authority to intercedefor others.

Woman's Calling in Christ

Who hath saved us, and called us with an holy calling, not according to our works, but according to his own purpose and grace, which was given us in Christ Jesus before the world began. 2 Timothy 1:9

I therefore, the prisoner of the Lord, beseech you that ye walk worthy of the vocation wherewith ye are called. Ephesians 4:1

Wherefore the rather, brethren, give diligence to make your calling and election sure: for if ye do these things, ye shall never fall.
2 Peter 1:10

And we know that all things work together for good to them that love God, to them who are the called according to his purpose.
Romans 8:28

For the gifts and calling of God are without repentance.
Romans 11:29

But ye are a chosen generation, a royal priesthood, an holy nation, a peculiar people; that ye should shewforth the praises of him who hath called you out of darkness into his marvellous light. 1 Peter 2:9

For by grace are ye saved through faith; and that not of yourselves: it is the gift of God: Not of works, lest any man should boast. For we are his workmanship, created in Christ Jesus unto good works, which God hath before ordained that we should walk in them. Ephesians 2:8-10

Let your light so shine before men, that they may see your good works, and glorify your Father which is in heaven. Matthew 5:16

Your calling in Christ is not a burden but a privilege—embrace it with joy and walk worthy of your high calling.

VESSELS OF HONOR

But in a great house there are not only vessels of gold and of silver, but also of wood and of earth; andsome to honour, and some to dishonour. If a man therefore purge himself from these, he shall be a vesselunto honour, sanctified, and meet for the master's use, and prepared unto every good work. 2 Timothy 2:20-21

But we have this treasure in earthen vessels, that the excellency of the power may be of God, and not ofus. 2 Corinthians 4:7

Likewise, ye wives, be in subjection to your own husbands; that, if any obey not the word, they also maywithout the word be won by the conversation of the wives; While they behold your chaste conversationcoupled with fear. Whose adorning let it not be that outward adorning of plaiting the hair, and of wearingof gold, or of putting on of apparel; But let it be the hidden man of the heart, in that which is not corruptible, even the ornament of a meek and quiet spirit, which is in the sight of God of great price. 1Peter 3:1-4

Hath not the potter power over the clay, of the same lump to make one vessel unto honour, and anotherunto dishonour? Romans 9:21

But now, O Lord, thou art our father; we are the clay, and thou our potter; and we all are the work of thyhand. Isaiah 64:8

I can do all things through Christ which strengtheneth me. Philippians 4:13

For it is God which worketh in you both to will and to do of his good pleasure. Philippians 2:13

You are God's chosen vessel, prepared and equipped for His honor and glory—let Him fill you anduse you.

Woman's Spiritual Inheritance

The Spirit itself beareth witness with our spirit, that we are the children of God: And if children, then heirs;heirs of God, and joint-heirs with Christ; if so be that we suffer with him, that we may be also glorifiedtogether. Romans 8:16-17

In whom also we have obtained an inheritance, being predestinated according to the purpose of himwho worketh all things after the counsel of his own will. Ephesians 1:11

Giving thanks unto the Father, which hath made us meet to be partakers of the inheritance of the saints inlight. Colossians 1:12

And if ye be Christ's, then are ye Abraham's seed, and heirs according to the promise. Galatians 3:29

Blessed be the God and Father of our Lord Jesus Christ, which according to his abundant mercy hathbegotten us again unto a lively hope by the resurrection of Jesus Christ from the dead, To an inheritanceincorruptible, and undefiled, and that fadeth not away, reserved in heaven for you. 1 Peter 1:3-4

That the Gentiles should be fellowheirs, and of the same body, and partakers of his promise in Christ bythe gospel. Ephesians 3:6
And this is the record, that God hath given to us eternal life, and this life is in his Son. 1 John 5:11

Whereby are given unto us exceeding great and precious promises: that by these ye might be partakersof the divine nature, having escaped the corruption that is in the world through lust. 2 Peter 1:4

Your spiritual inheritance in Christ is beyond measure—claim your inheritance as a daughter of theKing.

God's Masterpiece

For we are his workmanship, created in Christ Jesus unto good works, which God hath before ordainedthat we should walk in them. Ephesians 2:10

I will praise thee; for I am fearfully and wonderfully made: marvellous are thy works; and that my soulknoweth right well. Psalms 139:14

But now, O Lord, thou art our father; we are the clay, and thou our potter; and we all are the work of thyhand. Isaiah 64:8
So God created man in his own image, in the image of God created he him; male and female created hethem. Genesis 1:27

Before I formed thee in the belly I knew thee; and before thou camest forth out of the womb I sanctifiedthee, and I ordained thee a prophet unto the nations. Jeremiah 1:5

For thou hast possessed my reins: thou hast covered me in my mother's womb. My substance was nothid from thee, when I was made in secret, and curiously wrought in the lowest parts of the earth. Thineeyes did see my substance, yet being unperfect; and in thy book all my members were written, which incontinuance were fashioned, when as yet there was none of them. Psalms 139:13-16

The Lord will perfect that which concerneth me: thy mercy, O Lord, endureth for ever: forsake not theworks of thine own hands.
Psalms 138:8

Being confident of this very thing, that he which hath begun a good work in you will perform it until theday of Jesus Christ.
Philippians 1:6

You are God's masterpiece, His workmanship, carefully crafted with love and divine intention.

Woman as Light Bearer

Ye are the light of the world. A city that is set on an hill cannot be hid. Neither do men light a candle, andput it under a bushel, but on a candlestick; and it giveth light unto all that are in the house. Let your lightso shine before men, that they may see your good works, and glorify your Father which is in heaven.Matthew 5:14-16

But ye are a chosen generation, a royal priesthood, an holy nation, a peculiar people; that ye should shewforth the praises of him who hath called you out of darkness into his marvellous light. 1 Peter 2:9

For ye were sometimes darkness, but now are ye light in the Lord: walk as children of light: (For the fruitof the Spirit is in all goodness and righteousness and truth;) Proving what is acceptable unto the Lord.Ephesians 5:8-10

Then spake Jesus again unto them, saying, I am the light of the world: he that followeth me shall not walkin darkness, but shall have the light of life. John 8:12

And this is the condemnation, that light is come into the world, and men loved darkness rather than light,because their deeds were evil. For every one that doeth evil hateth the light, neither cometh to the light,lest his deeds should be reproved. But he that doeth truth cometh to the light, that his deeds may bemade manifest, that they are wrought in God. John 3:19-21

The night is far spent, the day is at hand: let us therefore cast off the works of darkness, and let us put onthe armour of light.
Romans 13:12

That ye may be blameless and harmless, the sons of God, without rebuke, in the midst of a crooked andperverse nation, among whom ye shine as lights in the world. Philippians 2:15

As a woman of God, you are called to be a light bearer, illuminating the darkness wherever Godplaces you.

Woman's Destiny

For I know the thoughts that I think toward you, saith the Lord, thoughts of peace, and not of evil, to give you an expected end. Jeremiah 29:11

And we know that all things work together for good to them that love God, to them who are the called according to his purpose.

For whom he did foreknow, he also did predestinate to be conformed to the image of his Son, that he might be the firstborn among many brethren. Romans 8:28-29

Being confident of this very thing, that he which hath begun a good work in you will perform it until the day of Jesus Christ. Philippians 1:6

The steps of a good man are ordered by the Lord: and he delighteth in his way. Psalms 37:23

Trust in the Lord with all thine heart; and lean not unto thine own understanding. In all thy ways acknowledge him, and he shall direct thy paths. Proverbs 3:5-6

For we are his workmanship, created in Christ Jesus unto good works, which God hath before ordained that we should walk in them. Ephesians 2:10

Who hath saved us, and called us with an holy calling, not according to our works, but according to his own purpose and grace, which was given us in Christ Jesus before the world began. 2 Timothy 1:9

Many are the plans in a man's heart, but it is the Lord's purpose that prevails. Proverbs 19:21

Your destiny as a woman is secure in God's hands—trust His timing and His perfect plan for your life.

God's Favor on Women

For thou, Lord, wilt bless the righteous; with favour wilt thou compass him as with a shield. Psalms 5:12

For his anger endureth but a moment; in his favour is life: weeping may endure for a night, but joycometh in the morning. Psalms 30:5

And Jesus increased in wisdom and stature, and in favour with God and man. Luke 2:52

Let not mercy and truth forsake thee: bind them about thy neck; write them upon the table of thine heart:So shalt thou find favour and good understanding in the sight of God and man. Proverbs 3:3-4

A good man obtaineth favour of the Lord: but a man of wicked devices will he condemn. Proverbs 12:2

And the angel came in unto her, and said, Hail, thou that art highly favoured, the Lord is with thee:blessed art thou among women. Luke 1:28

Whoso findeth a wife findeth a good thing, and obtaineth favour of the Lord. Proverbs 18:22

For thou hast made him most blessed for ever: thou hast made him exceeding glad with thycountenance. Psalms 21:6

Remember me, O Lord, with the favour that thou bearest unto thy people: O visit me with thy salvation.Psalms 106:4

God's favor rests upon you as His daughter—walk in the confidence of His blessing upon your life.

Woman's Divine Potential

Now unto him that is able to do exceeding abundantly above all that we ask or think, according to thepower that worketh in us.
Ephesians 3:20

I can do all things through Christ which strengtheneth me.
Philippians 4:13

For it is God which worketh in you both to will and to do of his good pleasure. Philippians 2:13
But my God shall supply all your need according to his riches in glory by Christ Jesus. Philippians 4:19

Greater is he that is in you, than he that is in the world. 1 John 4:4

Being confident of this very thing, that he which hath begun a good work in you will perform it until theday of Jesus Christ.
Philippians 1:6

For we are his workmanship, created in Christ Jesus unto good works, which God hath before ordainedthat we should walk in them.
Ephesians 2:10

Verily, verily, I say unto you, He that believeth on me, the works that I do shall he do also; and greaterworks than these shall he do; because I go unto my Father. John 14:12

And Jesus looking upon them saith, With men it is impossible, but not with God: for with God all thingsare possible. Mark 10:27

Your potential in God is limitless—don't settle for less than the extraordinary life He has plannedfor you.

Blessed Among Women

And the angel came in unto her, and said, Hail, thou that art highly favoured, the Lord is with thee:blessed art thou among women.
Luke 1:28

And it came to pass, that, when Elisabeth heard the salutation of Mary, the babe leaped in her womb; andElisabeth was filled with the Holy Ghost: And she spake out with a loud voice, and said, Blessed art thouamong women, and blessed is the fruit of thy womb.
Luke 1:41-42

Blessed is she that believed: for there shall be a performance of those things which were told her from theLord. Luke 1:45

And Mary said, My soul doth magnify the Lord, And my spirit hath rejoiced in God my Saviour. For hehath regarded the low estate of his handmaiden: for, behold, from henceforth all generations shall call meblessed. For he that is mighty hath done to me great things; and holy is his name. Luke 1:46-49

Many daughters have done virtuously, but thou excellest them all. Proverbs 31:29

Her children arise up, and call her blessed; her husband also, and he praiseth her. Proverbs 31:28

The king's daughter is all glorious within: her clothing is of wrought gold. Psalms 45:13

Favour is deceitful, and beauty is vain: but a woman that feareth the Lord, she shall be praised. Give her ofthe fruit of her hands; and let her own works praise her in the gates. Proverbs 31:30-31

You are blessed among women—chosen by God for a special purpose in His kingdom plan.

Woman's Sacred Mission

And Jesus came and spake unto them, saying, All power is given unto me in heaven and in earth. Go yetherefore, and teach all nations, baptizing them in the name of the Father, and of the Son, and of the HolyGhost: Teaching them to observe all things whatsoever I have commanded you: and, lo, I am with youalway, even unto the end of the world. Amen. Matthew 28:18-20

But ye shall receive power, after that the Holy Ghost is come upon you: and ye shall be witnesses unto meboth in Jerusalem, and in all Judaea, and in Samaria, and unto the uttermost part of the earth. Acts 1:8

For we are his workmanship, created in Christ Jesus unto good works, which God hath before ordainedthat we should walk in them. Ephesians 2:10

Ye are the light of the world. A city that is set on an hill cannot be hid. Let your light so shine before men,that they may see your good works, and glorify your Father which is in heaven. Matthew 5:14-16

And he said unto them, Go ye into all the world, and preach the gospel to every creature. Mark 16:15

The aged women likewise, that they be in behaviour as becometh holiness, not false accusers, not givento much wine, teachers of good things; That they may teach the young women to be sober, to love theirhusbands, to love their children. Titus 2:3-4

Pure religion and undefiled before God and the Father is this, To visit the fatherless and widows in theiraffliction, and to keep himself unspotted from the world. James 1:27

Your sacred mission as a woman is to reflect God's love, share His gospel, and disciple the nextgeneration.

SECTION II: CHARACTER & VIRTUE

The Proverbs 31 Woman

Who can find a virtuous woman? for her price is far above rubies. The heart of her husband doth safely trust in her, so that he shall have no need of spoil. She will do him good and not evil all the days of her life. She seeketh wool, and flax, and worketh willingly with her hands. She is like the merchants' ships; she bringeth her food from afar. She riseth also while it is yet night, and giveth meat to her household, and a portion to her maidens. She considereth a field, and buyeth it: with the fruit of her hands she planteth a vineyard. She girdeth her loins with strength, and strengtheneth her arms. She perceiveth that her merchandise is good: her candle goeth not out by night. She layeth her hands to the spindle, and her hands hold the distaff. She stretcheth out her hand to the poor; yea, she reacheth forth her hands to the needy. She is not afraid of the snow for her household: for all her household are clothed with scarlet. She maketh herself coverings of tapestry; her clothing is silk and purple. Her husband is known in the gates, when he sitteth among the elders of the land. She maketh fine linen, and selleth it; and delivereth girdles unto the merchant. Strength and honour are her clothing; and she shall rejoice in time to come. She openeth her mouth with wisdom; and in her tongue is the law of kindness. She looketh well to the ways of her household, and eateth not the bread of idleness. Her children arise up, and call her blessed; her husband also, and he praiseth her. Many daughters have done virtuously, but thou excellest them all.

Favour is deceitful, and beauty is vain: but a woman that feareth the Lord, she shall be praised. Give her of the fruit of her hands; and let her own works praise her in the gates. Proverbs 31:10-31

A gracious woman retaineth honour: and strong men retain riches. Proverbs 11:16

Every wise woman buildeth her house: but the foolish plucketh it down with her hands. Proverbs 14:1

House and riches are the inheritance of fathers: and a prudent wife is from the Lord. Proverbs 19:14

Whoso findeth a wife findeth a good thing, and obtaineth favour of the Lord. Proverbs 18:22

The Proverbs 31 woman is not a standard to strive for but a picture of what God can accomplishthrough a surrendered life.

Godly Character

But the fruit of the Spirit is love, joy, peace, longsuffering, gentleness, goodness, faith, Meekness,temperance: against such there is no law. Galatians 5:22-23

And beside this, giving all diligence, add to your faith virtue; and to virtue knowledge; And to knowledgetemperance; and to temperance patience; and to patience godliness; And to godliness brotherly kindness;and to brotherly kindness charity. For if these things be in you, and abound, they make you that ye shallneither be barren nor unfruitful in the knowledge of our Lord Jesus Christ. 2 Peter 1:5-8

Finally, brethren, whatsoever things are true, whatsoever things are honest, whatsoever things are just,whatsoever things are pure, whatsoever things are lovely, whatsoever things are of good report; if therebe any virtue, and if there be any praise, think on these things. Philippians 4:8

But thou, O man of God, flee these things; and follow after righteousness, godliness, faith, love, patience,meekness.
1 Timothy 6:11

And above all these things put on charity, which is the bond of perfectness. Colossians 3:14

Therefore if any man be in Christ, he is a new creature: old things are passed away; behold, all things arebecome new. 2 Corinthians 5:17

But as he which hath called you is holy, so be ye holy in all manner of conversation; Because it is written,Be ye holy; for I am holy.
1 Peter 1:15-16

That ye put off concerning the former conversation the old man, which is corrupt according to thedeceitful lusts; And be renewed in the spirit of your mind; And that ye put on the new man, which afterGod is created in righteousness and true holiness. Ephesians 4:22-24

Godly character is not achieved through human effort alone, but through the transforming powerof God's Spirit within.

Woman of Excellence

And whatsoever ye do, do it heartily, as to the Lord, and not unto men. Colossians 3:23

Whether therefore ye eat, or drink, or whatsoever ye do, do all to the glory of God. 1 Corinthians 10:31

She girdeth her loins with strength, and strengtheneth her arms. She perceiveth that her merchandise isgood: her candle goeth not out by night. Proverbs 31:17-18

Many daughters have done virtuously, but thou excellest them all. Proverbs 31:29

And that ye study to be quiet, and to do your own business, and to work with your own hands, as wecommanded you; That ye may walk honestly toward them that are without, and that ye may have lack ofnothing. 1 Thessalonians 4:11-12

Let us therefore follow after the things which make for peace, and things wherewith one may edifyanother. Romans 14:19

That ye might walk worthy of the Lord unto all pleasing, being fruitful in every good work, and increasingin the knowledge of God. Colossians 1:10

For we are his workmanship, created in Christ Jesus unto good works, which God hath before ordainedthat we should walk in them. Ephesians 2:10

And let us not be weary in well doing: for in due season we shall reap, if we faint not. Galatians 6:9

Excellence is not perfection—it's doing your best with what God has given you, for His glory.

Virtuous Woman

A virtuous woman is a crown to her husband: but she that maketh ashamed is as rottenness in his bones.Proverbs 12:4

Who can find a virtuous woman? for her price is far above rubies. Proverbs 31:10

Many daughters have done virtuously, but thou excellest them all. Proverbs 31:29

The aged women likewise, that they be in behaviour as becometh holiness, not false accusers, not givento much wine, teachers of good things; That they may teach the young women to be sober, to love theirhusbands, to love their children, To be discreet, chaste, keepers at home, good, obedient to their ownhusbands, that the word of God be not blasphemed. Titus 2:3-5

But the fruit of the Spirit is love, joy, peace, longsuffering, gentleness, goodness, faith, Meekness,temperance: against such there is no law. Galatians 5:22-23

Favour is deceitful, and beauty is vain: but a woman that feareth the Lord, she shall be praised. Proverbs 31:30

Likewise, ye wives, be in subjection to your own husbands; that, if any obey not the word, they also maywithout the word be won by the conversation of the wives; While they behold your chaste conversationcoupled with fear. 1 Peter 3:1-2

A gracious woman retaineth honour: and strong men retain riches. Proverbs 11:16

True virtue flows from a heart transformed by God's grace and submitted to His will and ways.

Noble Character

And beside this, giving all diligence, add to your faith virtue; and to virtue knowledge; And to knowledgetemperance; and to temperance patience; and to patience godliness; And to godliness brotherly kindness;and to brotherly kindness charity. 2 Peter 1:5-8

Finally, brethren, whatsoever things are true, whatsoever things are honest, whatsoever things are just,whatsoever things are pure, whatsoever things are lovely, whatsoever things are of good report; if therebe any virtue, and if there be any praise, think on these things. Philippians 4:8

Strength and honour are her clothing; and she shall rejoice in time to come. Proverbs 31:25

But as he which hath called you is holy, so be ye holy in all manner of conversation; Because it is written,Be ye holy; for I am holy.
1 Peter 1:15-16

Keep thy heart with all diligence; for out of it are the issues of life. Proverbs 4:23

But thou, O man of God, flee these things; and follow after righteousness, godliness, faith, love, patience,meekness.
1 Timothy 6:11

That ye might walk worthy of the Lord unto all pleasing, being fruitful in every good work, and increasingin the knowledge of God.
Colossians 1:10

And above all these things put on charity, which is the bond of perfectness. Colossians 3:14

The king's daughter is all glorious within: her clothing is of wrought gold. Psalms 45:13

Noble character is built through daily choices to honor God in both the seen and unseen momentsof life.

INNER BEAUTY

Whose adorning let it not be that outward adorning of plaiting the hair, and of wearing of gold, or ofputting on of apparel; But let it be the hidden man of the heart, in that which is not corruptible, even the ornament of a meek and quiet spirit, which is in the sight of God of great price. 1 Peter 3:3-4

The king's daughter is all glorious within: her clothing is of wrought gold. Psalms 45:13

Favour is deceitful, and beauty is vain: but a woman that feareth the Lord, she shall be praised. Proverbs31:30

For the Lord seeth not as man seeth; for man looketh on the outward appearance, but the Lord lookethon the heart. 1 Samuel 16:7

But the fruit of the Spirit is love, joy, peace, longsuffering, gentleness, goodness, faith, Meekness,temperance: against such there is no law. Galatians 5:22-23

And be not conformed to this world: but be ye transformed by the renewing of your mind, that ye mayprove what is that good, and acceptable, and perfect, will of God. Romans 12:2

Keep thy heart with all diligence; for out of it are the issues of life. Proverbs 4:23

That Christ may dwell in your hearts by faith; that ye, being rooted and grounded in love. Ephesians 3:17

True beauty radiates from within—cultivate your heart and let God's beauty shine through you.

Gentle and Quiet Spirit

But let it be the hidden man of the heart, in that which is not corruptible, even the ornament of a meekand quiet spirit, which is in the sight of God of great price. 1 Peter 3:4

Blessed are the meek: for they shall inherit the earth. Matthew 5:5

But the fruit of the Spirit is love, joy, peace, longsuffering, gentleness, goodness, faith, Meekness,temperance: against such there is no law. Galatians 5:22-23

Take my yoke upon you, and learn of me; for I am meek and lowly in heart: and ye shall find rest untoyour souls. Matthew 11:29

Let your moderation be known unto all men. The Lord is at hand. Philippians 4:5

But the wisdom that is from above is first pure, then peaceable, gentle, and easy to be intreated, full ofmercy and good fruits, without partiality, and without hypocrisy. James 3:17

And the servant of the Lord must not strive; but be gentle unto all men, apt to teach, patient. 2 Timothy2:24

But thou, O man of God, flee these things; and follow after righteousness, godliness, faith, love, patience,meekness.
1 Timothy 6:11

A soft answer turneth away wrath: but grievous words stir up anger. Proverbs 15:1

A gentle and quiet spirit is not weakness—it is strength under God's control.

Woman of Integrity

The integrity of the upright shall guide them: but the perverseness of transgressors shall destroy them.Proverbs 11:3

Let integrity and uprightness preserve me; for I wait on thee. Psalms 25:21

He that walketh uprightly walketh surely: but he that perverteth his ways shall be known. Proverbs 10:9

Better is the poor that walketh in his integrity, than he that is perverse in his lips, and is a fool. Proverbs19:1

Judge me, O Lord; for I have walked in mine integrity: I have trusted also in the Lord; therefore I shall notslide. Psalms 26:1

The just man walketh in his integrity: his children are blessed after him. Proverbs 20:7

And as for me, thou upholdest me in mine integrity, and settest me before thy face for ever. Psalms 41:12

A good name is rather to be chosen than great riches, and loving favour rather than silver and gold.Proverbs 22:1

Finally, brethren, whatsoever things are true, whatsoever things are honest, whatsoever things are just,whatsoever things are pure, whatsoever things are lovely, whatsoever things are of good report; if therebe any virtue, and if there be any praise, think on these things. Philippians 4:8

Integrity means being the same person in private that you are in public—authentic before Godand others.

Wisdom in Women

She openeth her mouth with wisdom; and in her tongue is the law of kindness. Proverbs 31:26

Every wise woman buildeth her house: but the foolish plucketh it down with her hands. Proverbs 14:1

The fear of the Lord is the beginning of wisdom: and the knowledge of the holy is understanding.Proverbs 9:10

If any of you lack wisdom, let him ask of God, that giveth to all men liberally, and upbraideth not; and itshall be given him. James 1:5

Happy is the man that findeth wisdom, and the man that getteth understanding. For the merchandise ofit is better than the merchandise of silver, and the gain thereof than fine gold. She is more precious thanrubies: and all the things thou canst desire are not to be compared unto her. Proverbs 3:13-15

Get wisdom, get understanding: forget it not; neither decline from the words of my mouth. Forsake hernot, and she shall preserve thee: love her, and she shall keep thee. Wisdom is the principal thing;therefore get wisdom: and with all thy getting get understanding.
Proverbs 4:5-7

But the wisdom that is from above is first pure, then peaceable, gentle, and easy to be intreated, full ofmercy and good fruits, without partiality, and without hypocrisy. James 3:17

Howbeit we speak wisdom among them that are perfect: yet not the wisdom of this world, nor of theprinces of this world, that come to nought: But we speak the wisdom of God in a mystery, even thehidden wisdom, which God ordained before the world unto our glory.
1 Corinthians 2:6-7

A wise woman seeks God's wisdom first and foremost, knowing it will guide every area of her life.

Discerning Woman

A wise man's heart discerneth both time and judgment. Ecclesiastes 8:5

The simple believeth every word: but the prudent man looketh well to his going. Proverbs 14:15

But strong meat belongeth to them that are of full age, even those who by reason of use have theirsenses exercised to discern both good and evil. Hebrews 5:14

Beloved, believe not every spirit, but try the spirits whether they are of God: because many false prophetsare gone out into the world.
1 John 4:1

Prove all things; hold fast that which is good. 1 Thessalonians 5:21

For this cause we also, since the day we heard it, do not cease to pray for you, and to desire that ye mightbe filled with the knowledge of his will in all wisdom and spiritual understanding. Colossians 1:9

Give therefore thy servant an understanding heart to judge thy people, that I may discern between goodand bad: for who is able to judge this thy so great a people? 1 Kings 3:9

And this I pray, that your love may abound yet more and more in knowledge and in all judgment; That yemay approve things that are excellent; that ye may be sincere and without offence till the day of Christ.Philippians 1:9-10

But the wisdom that is from above is first pure, then peaceable, gentle, and easy to be intreated, full ofmercy and good fruits, without partiality, and without hypocrisy. James 3:17

A discerning woman can distinguish between truth and error, wisdom and foolishness, throughGod's Spirit within her.

Woman of Faith

Now faith is the substance of things hoped for, the evidence of things not seen. Hebrews 11:1

But without faith it is impossible to please him: for he that cometh to God must believe that he is, andthat he is a rewarder of them that diligently seek him. Hebrews 11:6

And Jesus answering saith unto them, Have faith in God. For verily I say unto you, That whosoever shallsay unto this mountain, Be thou removed, and be thou cast into the sea; and shall not doubt in his heart,but shall believe that those things which he saith shall come to pass; he shall have whatsoever he saith.Mark 11:22-23

Jesus said unto him, If thou canst believe, all things are possible to him that believeth. Mark 9:23

So then faith cometh by hearing, and hearing by the word of God. Romans 10:17

For we walk by faith, not by sight. 2 Corinthians 5:7

Looking unto Jesus the author and finisher of our faith; who for the joy that was set before him enduredthe cross, despising the shame, and is set down at the right hand of the throne of God. Hebrews 12:2

And the prayer of faith shall save the sick, and the Lord shall raise him up; and if he have committed sins,they shall be forgiven him. James 5:15

For whatsoever is born of God overcometh the world: and this is the victory that overcometh the world,even our faith. 1 John 5:4

Faith is not the absence of questions or doubts—it is trusting God in spite of them. - ElisabethElliot

Courageous Woman

Be strong and of a good courage; be not afraid, neither be thou dismayed: for the Lord thy God is withthee whithersoever thou goest. Joshua 1:9

Have not I commanded thee? Be strong and of a good courage; be not afraid, neither be thou dismayed:for the Lord thy God is with thee whithersoever thou goest. Joshua 1:9

The wicked flee when no man pursueth: but the righteous are bold as a lion. Proverbs 28:1

Wait on the Lord: be of good courage, and he shall strengthen thine heart: wait, I say, on the Lord. Psalms 27:14

In God have I put my trust: I will not be afraid what man can do unto me. Psalms 56:11

And who knoweth whether thou art come to the kingdom for such a time as this? Esther 4:14

Be of good courage, and he shall strengthen your heart, all ye that hope in the Lord. Psalms 31:24

I can do all things through Christ which strengtheneth me. Philippians 4:13

For God hath not given us the spirit of fear; but of power, and of love, and of a sound mind. 2 Timothy 1:7

Fear thou not; for I am with thee: be not dismayed; for I am thy God: I will strengthen thee; yea, I will helpthee; yea, I will uphold thee with the right hand of my righteousness. Isaiah 41:10

Courage is not the absence of fear—it is moving forward in spite of it.

Strong Woman

She girdeth her loins with strength, and strengtheneth her arms. Proverbs 31:17

Strength and honour are her clothing; and she shall rejoice in time to come. Proverbs 31:25

The Lord is my strength and my shield; my heart trusted in him, and I am helped: therefore my heartgreatly rejoiceth; and with my song will I praise him. Psalms 28:7

I can do all things through Christ which strengtheneth me. Philippians 4:13

But they that wait upon the Lord shall renew their strength; they shall mount up with wings as eagles;they shall run, and not be weary; and they shall walk, and not faint. Isaiah 40:31

The Lord is my strength and song, and he is become my salvation: he is my God, and I will prepare him anhabitation; my father's God, and I will exalt him. Exodus 15:2

Be strong in the Lord, and in the power of his might. Ephesians 6:10
Finally, my brethren, be strong in the Lord, and in the power of his might. Ephesians 6:10

He giveth power to the faint; and to them that have no might he increaseth strength. Isaiah 40:29

For when I am weak, then am I strong. 2 Corinthians 12:10

True strength comes not from physical might but from dependence on God's power within you.

COMPASSIONATE HEART

And be ye kind one to another, tenderhearted, forgiving one another, even as God for Christ's sake hathforgiven you. Ephesians 4:32

But the fruit of the Spirit is love, joy, peace, longsuffering, gentleness, goodness, faith. Galatians 5:22

Put on therefore, as the elect of God, holy and beloved, bowels of mercies, kindness, humbleness of mind,meekness, longsuffering. Colossians 3:12

She stretcheth out her hand to the poor; yea, she reacheth forth her hands to the needy. Proverbs 31:20

Be pitiful, be courteous. 1 Peter 3:8

Finally, be ye all of one mind, having compassion one of another, love as brethren, be pitiful, becourteous. 1 Peter 3:8

But whoso hath this world's good, and seeth his brother have need, and shutteth up his bowels ofcompassion from him, how dwelleth the love of God in him? 1 John 3:17

Can a woman forget her sucking child, that she should not have compassion on the son of her womb?yea, they may forget, yet will I not forget thee. Isaiah 49:15

And Jesus, when he came out, saw much people, and was moved with compassion toward them, becausethey were as sheep not having a shepherd: and he began to teach them many things. Mark 6:34

A compassionate heart reflects the very heart of God—let His love flow through you to a hurtingworld.

GRACIOUS WOMAN

A gracious woman retaineth honour: and strong men retain riches. Proverbs 11:16

She openeth her mouth with wisdom; and in her tongue is the law of kindness. Proverbs 31:26

Let your speech be alway with grace, seasoned with salt, that ye may know how ye ought to answer everyman. Colossians 4:6

A soft answer turneth away wrath: but grievous words stir up anger. Proverbs 15:1

But the fruit of the Spirit is love, joy, peace, longsuffering, gentleness, goodness, faith, Meekness,temperance: against such there is no law. Galatians 5:22-23

Pleasant words are as an honeycomb, sweet to the soul, and health to the bones. Proverbs 16:24

Let no corrupt communication proceed out of your mouth, but that which is good to the use of edifying,that it may minister grace unto the hearers. Ephesians 4:29

And be ye kind one to another, tenderhearted, forgiving one another, even as God for Christ's sake hathforgiven you. Ephesians 4:32

By long forbearing is a prince persuaded, and a soft tongue breaketh the bone. Proverbs 25:15

Grace in speech and manner opens doors that force cannot open and wins hearts that aggressioncannot touch.

Patient Woman

But the fruit of the Spirit is love, joy, peace, longsuffering, gentleness, goodness, faith. Galatians 5:22

Rest in the Lord, and wait patiently for him: fret not thyself because of him who prospereth in his way,because of the man who bringeth wicked devices to pass. Psalms 37:7

But let patience have her perfect work, that ye may be perfect and entire, wanting nothing. James 1:4

Be patient therefore, brethren, unto the coming of the Lord. Behold, the husbandman waiteth for theprecious fruit of the earth, and hath long patience for it, until he receive the early and latter rain. Be yealso patient; stablish your hearts: for the coming of the Lord draweth nigh. James 5:7-8

And we desire that every one of you do shew the same diligence to the full assurance of hope unto theend: That ye be not slothful, but followers of them who through faith and patience inherit the promises.Hebrews 6:11-12

In your patience possess ye your souls. Luke 21:19

With all lowliness and meekness, with longsuffering, forbearing one another in love. Ephesians 4:2

For ye have need of patience, that, after ye have done the will of God, ye might receive the promise.Hebrews 10:36

Patience is not passive waiting—it is active trust in God's perfect timing.

Humble Heart

Humble yourselves therefore under the mighty hand of God, that he may exalt you in due time. 1 Peter5:6

Likewise, ye younger, submit yourselves unto the elder. Yea, all of you be subject one to another, and beclothed with humility: for God resisteth the proud, and giveth grace to the humble. 1 Peter 5:5

But he giveth more grace. Wherefore he saith, God resisteth the proud, but giveth grace unto thehumble. James 4:6

Pride goeth before destruction, and an haughty spirit before a fall. Better it is to be of an humble spiritwith the lowly, than to divide the spoil with the proud. Proverbs 16:18-19

Take my yoke upon you, and learn of me; for I am meek and lowly in heart: and ye shall find rest untoyour souls. Matthew 11:29

Blessed are the poor in spirit: for theirs is the kingdom of heaven. Matthew 5:3

By humility and the fear of the Lord are riches, and honour, and life. Proverbs 22:4

And whosoever shall exalt himself shall be abased; and he that shall humble himself shall be exalted.Matthew 23:12

But the fruit of the Spirit is love, joy, peace, longsuffering, gentleness, goodness, faith, Meekness,temperance: against such there is no law. Galatians 5:22-23

Humility is not thinking less of yourself—it is thinking of yourself less. - C.S. Lewis

Self-Control for Women

But the fruit of the Spirit is love, joy, peace, longsuffering, gentleness, goodness, faith, Meekness,temperance: against such there is no law. Galatians 5:22-23

And beside this, giving all diligence, add to your faith virtue; and to virtue knowledge; And to knowledgetemperance; and to temperance patience; and to patience godliness. 2 Peter 1:5-6

He that hath no rule over his own spirit is like a city that is broken down, and without walls. Proverbs25:28

He that is slow to anger is better than the mighty; and he that ruleth his spirit than he that taketh a city.Proverbs 16:32

But I keep under my body, and bring it into subjection: lest that by any means, when I have preached toothers, I myself should be a castaway. 1 Corinthians 9:27

Teaching us that, denying ungodliness and worldly lusts, we should live soberly, righteously, and godly, inthis present world. Titus 2:12

Therefore gird up the loins of your mind, be sober, and hope to the end for the grace that is to bebrought unto you at the revelation of Jesus Christ. 1 Peter 1:13

The aged women likewise, that they be in behaviour as becometh holiness, not false accusers, not givento much wine, teachers of good things. Titus 2:3

Self-control is the Spirit's power working through your will to choose God's way over your naturalinclinations.

Contentment in Women

But godliness with contentment is great gain. For we brought nothing into this world, and it is certain wecan carry nothing out. And having food and raiment let us be therewith content. 1 Timothy 6:6-8

Not that I speak in respect of want: for I have learned, in whatsoever state I am, therewith to be content. Iknow both how to be abased, and I know how to abound: every where and in all things I am instructedboth to be full and to be hungry, both to abound and to suffer need. I can do all things through Christwhich strengtheneth me. Philippians 4:11-13

Let your conversation be without covetousness; and be content with such things as ye have: for he hathsaid, I will never leave thee, nor forsake thee. Hebrews 13:5

Better is an handful with quietness, than both the hands full with travail and vexation of spirit. Ecclesiastes 4:6

A sound heart is the life of the flesh: but envy the rottenness of the bones. Proverbs 14:30

Rest in the Lord, and wait patiently for him: fret not thyself because of him who prospereth in his way,because of the man who bringeth wicked devices to pass. Psalms 37:7

But my God shall supply all your need according to his riches in glory by Christ Jesus. Philippians 4:19

Delight thyself also in the Lord; and he shall give thee the desires of thine heart. Psalms 37:4

Contentment is not settling for less—it is finding satisfaction in God's provision and timing.

THANKFUL HEART

In every thing give thanks: for this is the will of God in Christ Jesus concerning you. 1 Thessalonians 5:18

O give thanks unto the Lord; for he is good: because his mercy endureth for ever. Psalms 118:1

Giving thanks always for all things unto God and the Father in the name of our Lord Jesus Christ.Ephesians 5:20

And let the peace of God rule in your hearts, to the which also ye are called in one body; and be yethankful. Colossians 3:15

Be careful for nothing; but in every thing by prayer and supplication with thanksgiving let your requestsbe made known unto God. Philippians 4:6

Continue in prayer, and watch in the same with thanksgiving. Colossians 4:2

I will praise thee, O Lord, with my whole heart; I will shew forth all thy marvellous works. Psalms 9:1

Enter into his gates with thanksgiving, and into his courts with praise: be thankful unto him, and bless hisname. Psalms 100:4

And whatsoever ye do in word or deed, do all in the name of the Lord Jesus, giving thanks to God andthe Father by him. Colossians 3:17

A thankful heart is a magnet for miracles—gratitude transforms your perspective and draws God'sblessings.

Pure Heart

Blessed are the pure in heart: for they shall see God. Matthew 5:8
Create in me a clean heart, O God; and renew a right spirit within me. Psalms 51:10

Who shall ascend into the hill of the Lord? or who shall stand in his holy place? He that hath clean hands,and a pure heart; who hath not lifted up his soul unto vanity, nor sworn deceitfully. Psalms 24:3-4

Unto the pure all things are pure: but unto them that are defiled and unbelieving is nothing pure; buteven their mind and conscience is defiled. Titus 1:15

Finally, brethren, whatsoever things are true, whatsoever things are honest, whatsoever things are just,whatsoever things are pure, whatsoever things are lovely, whatsoever things are of good report; if therebe any virtue, and if there be any praise, think on these things. Philippians 4:8

Keep thy heart with all diligence; for out of it are the issues of life. Proverbs 4:23

But as he which hath called you is holy, so be ye holy in all manner of conversation; Because it is written,Be ye holy; for I am holy.
1 Peter 1:15-16

Flee also youthful lusts: but follow righteousness, faith, charity, peace, with them that call on the Lord outof a pure heart. 2 Timothy 2:22

A pure heart seeks God above all else and finds Him in every circumstance of life.

Merciful Woman

Blessed are the merciful: for they shall obtain mercy. Matthew 5:7

But the wisdom that is from above is first pure, then peaceable, gentle, and easy to be intreated, full ofmercy and good fruits, without partiality, and without hypocrisy. James 3:17

Be ye therefore merciful, as your Father also is merciful. Luke 6:36

And be ye kind one to another, tenderhearted, forgiving one another, even as God for Christ's sake hathforgiven you. Ephesians 4:32

She stretcheth out her hand to the poor; yea, she reacheth forth her hands to the needy. Proverbs 31:20

Put on therefore, as the elect of God, holy and beloved, bowels of mercies, kindness, humbleness of mind,meekness, longsuffering. Colossians 3:12

For he shall have judgment without mercy, that hath shewed no mercy; and mercy rejoiceth againstjudgment. James 2:13

The merciful man doeth good to his own soul: but he that is cruel troubleth his own flesh. Proverbs 11:17

He hath shewed thee, O man, what is good; and what doth the Lord require of thee, but to do justly, andto love mercy, and to walk humbly with thy God? Micah 6:8

Mercy is love in action—it sees the need and responds with compassion.

Peacemaking Woman

Blessed are the peacemakers: for they shall be called the children of God. Matthew 5:9

But the wisdom that is from above is first pure, then peaceable, gentle, and easy to be intreated, full ofmercy and good fruits, without partiality, and without hypocrisy. And the fruit of righteousness is sown inpeace of them that make peace. James 3:17-18

If it be possible, as much as lieth in you, live peaceably with all men. Romans 12:18

Let us therefore follow after the things which make for peace, and things wherewith one may edifyanother. Romans 14:19

But the fruit of the Spirit is love, joy, peace, longsuffering, gentleness, goodness, faith. Galatians 5:22

A soft answer turneth away wrath: but grievous words stir up anger. Proverbs 15:1

And above all these things put on charity, which is the bond of perfectness. And let the peace of God rulein your hearts, to the which also ye are called in one body; and be ye thankful. Colossians 3:14-15

Depart from evil, and do good; seek peace, and pursue it.
Psalms 34:14

Salt is good: but if the salt have lost his saltness, wherewith will ye season it? Have salt in yourselves, andhave peace one with another. Mark 9:50

Peacemaking is not avoiding conflict—it is actively working toward reconciliation and unity.

Righteous Woman

But seek ye first the kingdom of God, and his righteousness; and all these things shall be added unto you. Matthew 6:33

The righteous shall flourish like the palm tree: he shall grow like a cedar in Lebanon. Psalms 92:12

For the righteous Lord loveth righteousness; his countenance doth behold the upright. Psalms 11:7

The wicked flee when no man pursueth: but the righteous are bold as a lion. Proverbs 28:1

The righteous is more excellent than his neighbour: but the way of the wicked seduceth them. Proverbs 12:26

But the path of the just is as the shining light, that shineth more and more unto the perfect day. Proverbs 4:18

Being filled with the fruits of righteousness, which are by Jesus Christ, unto the glory and praise of God. Philippians 1:11

For he hath made him to be sin for us, who knew no sin; that we might be made the righteousness of God in him. 2 Corinthians 5:21

And be found in him, not having mine own righteousness, which is of the law, but that which is through the faith of Christ, the righteousness which is of God by faith. Philippians 3:9

True righteousness is not our own goodness but Christ's righteousness lived out through us.

HOLY LIVING FOR WOMEN

But as he which hath called you is holy, so be ye holy in all manner of conversation; Because it is written,Be ye holy; for I am holy.
1 Peter 1:15-16

Follow peace with all men, and holiness, without which no man shall see the Lord. Hebrews 12:14

And be not conformed to this world: but be ye transformed by the renewing of your mind, that ye mayprove what is that good, and acceptable, and perfect, will of God. Romans 12:2

I beseech you therefore, brethren, by the mercies of God, that ye present your bodies a living sacrifice,holy, acceptable unto God, which is your reasonable service. Romans 12:1

Having therefore these promises, dearly beloved, let us cleanse ourselves from all filthiness of the fleshand spirit, perfecting holiness in the fear of God. 2 Corinthians 7:1

Know ye not that ye are the temple of God, and that the Spirit of God dwelleth in you? If any man defilethe temple of God, him shall God destroy; for the temple of God is holy, which temple ye are. 1Corinthians 3:16-17

That he might sanctify and cleanse it with the washing of water by the word, That he might present it tohimself a glorious church, not having spot, or wrinkle, or any such thing; but that it should be holy andwithout blemish. Ephesians 5:26-27

The aged women likewise, that they be in behaviour as becometh holiness, not false accusers, not givento much wine, teachers of good things. Titus 2:3

Holy living is not perfection but progression—daily yielding to God's transforming work in yourlife.

SECTION III: RELATIONSHIPS

Marriage and Wives

Wives, submit yourselves unto your own husbands, as unto the Lord. For the husband is the head of the wife, even as Christ is the head of the church: and he is the saviour of the body. Therefore as the church is subject unto Christ, so let the wives be to their own husbands in every thing. Husbands, love your wives, even as Christ also loved the church, and gave himself for it; That he might sanctify and cleanse it with the washing of water by the word, That he might present it to himself a glorious church, not having spot, or wrinkle, or any such thing; but that it should be holy and without blemish. So ought men to love their wives as their own bodies. He that loveth his wife loveth himself. For no man ever yet hated his own flesh; but nourisheth and cherisheth it, even as the Lord the church: For we are members of his body, of his flesh, and of his bones. For this cause shall a man leave his father and mother, and shall be joined unto his wife, and they two shall be one flesh. This is a great mystery: but I speak concerning Christ and the church. Nevertheless let every one of you in particular so love his wife even as himself; and the wife see that she reverence her husband. Ephesians 5:22-33

Likewise, ye wives, be in subjection to your own husbands; that, if any obey not the word, they also may without the word be won by the conversation of the wives; While they behold your chaste conversation coupled with fear. Whose adorning let it not be that outward adorning of plaiting the hair, and of wearing of gold, or of putting on of apparel; But let it be the hidden man of the heart, in that which is not corruptible, even the ornament of a meek and quiet spirit, which is in the sight of God of great price. For after this manner in the old time the holy women also, who trusted in God, adorned themselves, being in subjection unto their own husbands: Even as Sara obeyed Abraham, calling him lord: whose daughters ye are, as long as ye do well, and are not afraid with any amazement. Likewise, ye husbands, dwell with them according to knowledge, giving honour unto the wife, as unto the weaker vessel, and as being heirs together of the grace of life; that your prayers be not hindered. 1 Peter 3:1-7

Wives, submit yourselves unto your own husbands, as it is fit in the Lord. Husbands, love your wives, andbe not bitter against them. Colossians 3:18-19

The heart of her husband doth safely trust in her, so that he shall have no need of spoil. She will do himgood and not evil all the days of her life. Proverbs 31:11-12

A virtuous woman is a crown to her husband: but she that maketh ashamed is as rottenness in his bones.Proverbs 12:4

House and riches are the inheritance of fathers: and a prudent wife is from the Lord. Proverbs 19:14

Whoso findeth a wife findeth a good thing, and obtaineth favour of the Lord. Proverbs 18:22

Marriage is God's design for two people to become one, reflecting Christ's love for the churchthrough sacrificial love.

Single Woman's Life

I would that all men were even as I myself. But every man hath his proper gift of God, one after thismanner, and another after that. I say therefore to the unmarried and widows, It is good for them if theyabide even as I. But if they cannot contain, let them marry: for it is better to marry than to burn. 1Corinthians 7:7-9

There is difference also between a wife and a virgin. The unmarried woman careth for the things of theLord, that she may be holy both in body and in spirit: but she that is married careth for the things of theworld, how she may please her husband. 1 Corinthians 7:34

For thy Maker is thine husband; the Lord of hosts is his name; and thy Redeemer the Holy One of Israel;The God of the whole earth shall he be called. Isaiah 54:5

Trust in the Lord with all thine heart; and lean not unto thine own understanding. In all thy waysacknowledge him, and he shall direct thy paths. Proverbs 3:5-6

Delight thyself also in the Lord; and he shall give thee the desires of thine heart. Psalms 37:4

But my God shall supply all your need according to his riches in glory by Christ Jesus. Philippians 4:19

And Jesus answered and said, Verily I say unto you, There is no man that hath left house, or brethren, orsisters, or father, or mother, or wife, or children, or lands, for my sake, and the gospel's, But he shallreceive an hundredfold now in this time, houses, and brethren, and sisters, and mothers, and children,and lands, with persecutions; and in the world to come eternal life. Mark 10:29-30

I can do all things through Christ which strengtheneth me. Philippians 4:13

Singleness is not a consolation prize—it is a gift that allows complete devotion to God's purposes.

Sisterhood and Friendship

A friend loveth at all times, and a brother is born for adversity. Proverbs 17:17

Iron sharpeneth iron; so a man sharpeneth the countenance of his friend. Proverbs 27:17

Two are better than one; because they have a good reward for their labour. For if they fall, the one will liftup his fellow: but woe to him that is alone when he falleth; for he hath not another to help him up. Again,if two lie together, then they have heat: but how can one be warm alone? And if one prevail against him,two shall withstand him; and a threefold cord is not quickly broken. Ecclesiastes 4:9-12

Ointment and perfume rejoice the heart: so doth the sweetness of a man's friend by hearty counsel.Proverbs 27:9

Greater love hath no man than this, that a man lay down his life for his friends. Ye are my friends, if ye dowhatsoever I command you. Henceforth I call you not servants; for the servant knoweth not what his lorddoeth: but I have called you friends; for all things that I have heard of my Father I have made known untoyou. John 15:13-15

And Jonathan and David made a covenant, because he loved him as his own soul. 1 Samuel 18:3

Faithful are the wounds of a friend; but the kisses of an enemy are deceitful. Proverbs 27:6

Be kindly affectioned one to another with brotherly love; in honour preferring one another. Romans 12:10

A man that hath friends must shew himself friendly: and there is a friend that sticketh closer than abrother. Proverbs 18:24

True sisterhood in Christ creates bonds that strengthen, encourage, and sharpen one another forGod's glory.

Mother-Daughter Relationships

Her children arise up, and call her blessed; her husband also, and he praiseth her. Proverbs 31:28

Honour thy father and thy mother: that thy days may be long upon the land which the Lord thy Godgiveth thee. Exodus 20:12

Hearken unto thy father that begat thee, and despise not thy mother when she is old. Proverbs 23:22

My son, hear the instruction of thy father, and forsake not the law of thy mother: For they shall be anornament of grace unto thy head, and chains about thy neck. Proverbs 1:8-9

Children, obey your parents in the Lord: for this is right. Honour thy father and mother; which is the firstcommandment with promise; That it may be well with thee, and thou mayest live long on the earth. Ephesians 6:1-3

The proverbs of Solomon. A wise son maketh a glad father: but a foolish son is the heaviness of hismother. Proverbs 10:1

Train up a child in the way he should go: and when he is old, he will not depart from it. Proverbs 22:6

The aged women likewise, that they be in behaviour as becometh holiness, not false accusers, not givento much wine, teachers of good things; That they may teach the young women to be sober, to love theirhusbands, to love their children. Titus 2:3-4

A wise son heareth his father's instruction: but a scorner heareth not rebuke. Proverbs 13:1

The mother-daughter relationship is a sacred bond designed to pass down wisdom, faith, andgodly heritage.

Mentoring Women

The aged women likewise, that they be in behaviour as becometh holiness, not false accusers, not givento much wine, teachers of good things; That they may teach the young women to be sober, to love theirhusbands, to love their children, To be discreet, chaste, keepers at home, good, obedient to their ownhusbands, that the word of God be not blasphemed. Titus 2:3-5

And the things that thou hast heard of me among many witnesses, the same commit thou to faithfulmen, who shall be able to teach others also. 2 Timothy 2:2

Iron sharpeneth iron; so a man sharpeneth the countenance of his friend. Proverbs 27:17

Let the word of Christ dwell in you richly in all wisdom; teaching and admonishing one another in psalmsand hymns and spiritual songs, singing with grace in your hearts to the Lord. Colossians 3:16

Take my yoke upon you, and learn of me; for I am meek and lowly in heart: and ye shall find rest untoyour souls. Matthew 11:29

Remember them which have the rule over you, who have spoken unto you the word of God: whose faithfollow, considering the end of their conversation. Hebrews 13:7

Likewise, ye younger, submit yourselves unto the elder. Yea, all of you be subject one to another, and beclothed with humility: for God resisteth the proud, and giveth grace to the humble. 1 Peter 5:5

The lips of the righteous feed many: but fools die for want of wisdom. Proverbs 10:21

Mentoring is a sacred investment—pouring your life into another woman for the glory of God.

Community of Women

And they continued stedfastly in the apostles' doctrine and fellowship, and in breaking of bread, and inprayers. Acts 2:42

Not forsaking the assembling of ourselves together, as the manner of some is; but exhorting one another:and so much the more, as ye see the day approaching. Hebrews 10:25

Bear ye one another's burdens, and so fulfil the law of Christ. Galatians 6:2

And let us consider one another to provoke unto love and to good works. Hebrews 10:24

Confess your faults one to another, and pray one for another, that ye may be healed. The effectual ferventprayer of a righteous man availeth much. James 5:16

Two are better than one; because they have a good reward for their labour. For if they fall, the one will liftup his fellow: but woe to him that is alone when he falleth; for he hath not another to help him up.Ecclesiastes 4:9-10

As we have therefore opportunity, let us do good unto all men, especially unto them who are of thehousehold of faith. Galatians 6:10

For where two or three are gathered together in my name, there am I in the midst of them. Matthew18:20

Be kindly affectioned one to another with brotherly love; in honour preferring one another. Romans 12:10

Community among women creates a safe haven where hearts can be vulnerable, burdens shared,and spirits strengthened.

Submission in Marriage

Wives, submit yourselves unto your own husbands, as unto the Lord. For the husband is the head of thewife, even as Christ is the head of the church: and he is the saviour of the body. Therefore as the church issubject unto Christ, so let the wives be to their own husbands in every thing. Ephesians 5:22-24

Likewise, ye wives, be in subjection to your own husbands; that, if any obey not the word, they also maywithout the word be won by the conversation of the wives; While they behold your chaste conversationcoupled with fear. 1 Peter 3:1-2

Wives, submit yourselves unto your own husbands, as it is fit in the Lord. Colossians 3:18

For after this manner in the old time the holy women also, who trusted in God, adorned themselves,being in subjection unto their own husbands: Even as Sara obeyed Abraham, calling him lord: whosedaughters ye are, as long as ye do well, and are not afraid with any amazement. 1 Peter 3:5-6

Submit yourselves one to another in the fear of God. Ephesians 5:21

Whose adorning let it not be that outward adorning of plaiting the hair, and of wearing of gold, or ofputting on of apparel; But let it be the hidden man of the heart, in that which is not corruptible, even theornament of a meek and quiet spirit, which is in the sight of God of great price. 1 Peter 3:3-4

The heart of her husband doth safely trust in her, so that he shall have no need of spoil. She will do himgood and not evil all the days of her life. Proverbs 31:11-12

Biblical submission is not inferiority—it is a wife's willing choice to honor God's design formarriage.

Helpmeet and Partnership

And the Lord God said, It is not good that the man should be alone; I will make him an help meet for him.Genesis 2:18

And the rib, which the Lord God had taken from man, made he a woman, and brought her unto the man.And Adam said, This is now bone of my bones, and flesh of my flesh: she shall be called Woman, becauseshe was taken out of Man.

Therefore shall a man leave his father and his mother, and shall cleave unto hiswife: and they shall be one flesh. Genesis 2:22-24

Nevertheless neither is the man without the woman, neither the woman without the man, in the Lord. Foras the woman is of the man, even so is the man also by the woman; but all things of God. 1 Corinthians11:11-12

Two are better than one; because they have a good reward for their labour. For if they fall, the one will liftup his fellow: but woe to him that is alone when he falleth; for he hath not another to help him up.Ecclesiastes 4:9-10

The heart of her husband doth safely trust in her, so that he shall have no need of spoil. She will do himgood and not evil all the days of her life. Proverbs 31:11-12

Likewise, ye husbands, dwell with them according to knowledge, giving honour unto the wife, as unto theweaker vessel, and as being heirs together of the grace of life; that your prayers be not hindered. 1 Peter3:7

Whoso findeth a wife findeth a good thing, and obtaineth favour of the Lord. Proverbs 18:22

Marriage is a divine partnership where two become one, complementing each other in God'sperfect design.

Conflict Resolution

Moreover if thy brother shall trespass against thee, go and tell him his fault between thee and him alone:if he shall hear thee, thou hast gained thy brother. But if he will not hear thee, then take with thee one ortwo more, that in the mouth of two or three witnesses every word may be established. And if he shallneglect to hear them, tell it unto the church: but if he neglect to hear the church, let him be unto thee asan heathen man and a publican. Matthew 18:15-17

Be ye angry, and sin not: let not the sun go down upon your wrath. Ephesians 4:26

A soft answer turneth away wrath: but grievous words stir up anger. Proverbs 15:1

If it be possible, as much as lieth in you, live peaceably with all men. Romans 12:18

Blessed are the peacemakers: for they shall be called the children of God. Matthew 5:9

Forbearing one another, and forgiving one another, if any man have a quarrel against any: even as Christforgave you, so also do ye. Colossians 3:13

And above all these things put on charity, which is the bond of perfectness. Colossians 3:14

Let us therefore follow after the things which make for peace, and things wherewith one may edifyanother. Romans 14:19

The discretion of a man deferreth his anger; and it is his glory to pass over a transgression. Proverbs 19:11

Conflict resolution requires humility, grace, and a commitment to unity over being right.

Forgiveness in Relationships

And be ye kind one to another, tenderhearted, forgiving one another, even as God for Christ's sake hathforgiven you. Ephesians 4:32

Forbearing one another, and forgiving one another, if any man have a quarrel against any: even as Christforgave you, so also do ye. Colossians 3:13

Then came Peter to him, and said, Lord, how oft shall my brother sin against me, and I forgive him? tillseven times? Jesus saith unto him, I say not unto thee, Until seven times: but, Until seventy times seven. Matthew 18:21-22

And when ye stand praying, forgive, if ye have ought against any: that your Father also which is in heavenmay forgive you your trespasses. But if ye do not forgive, neither will your Father which is in heavenforgive your trespasses. Mark 11:25-26

Judge not, and ye shall not be judged: condemn not, and ye shall not be condemned: forgive, and yeshall be forgiven. Luke 6:37

And forgive us our debts, as we forgive our debtors. Matthew 6:12

But I say unto you, Love your enemies, bless them that curse you, do good to them that hate you, andpray for them which despitefully use you, and persecute you. Matthew 5:44

The discretion of a man deferreth his anger; and it is his glory to pass over a transgression. Proverbs 19:11

Forgiveness is not excusing the offense—it is releasing the offender for your own freedom andhealing.

Love and Romance

Let him kiss me with the kisses of his mouth: for thy love is better than wine. Song of Solomon 1:2

I am my beloved's, and my beloved is mine: he feedeth among the lilies. Song of Solomon 6:3

Many waters cannot quench love, neither can the floods drown it: if a man would give all the substance ofhis house for love, it would utterly be contemned. Song of Solomon 8:7

Set me as a seal upon thine heart, as a seal upon thine arm: for love is strong as death; jealousy is cruel asthe grave: the coals thereof are coals of fire, which hath a most vehement flame.
Song of Solomon 8:6

Charity suffereth long, and is kind; charity envieth not; charity vaunteth not itself, is not puffed up, Dothnot behave itself unseemly, seeketh not her own, is not easily provoked, thinketh no evil; Rejoiceth not ininiquity, but rejoiceth in the truth; Beareth all things, believeth all things, hopeth all things, endureth allthings. Charity never faileth. 1 Corinthians 13:4-8

Husbands, love your wives, even as Christ also loved the church, and gave himself for it. Ephesians 5:25

Live joyfully with the wife whom thou lovest all the days of the life of thy vanity, which he hath given theeunder the sun, all the days of thy vanity: for that is thy portion in this life, and in thy labour which thoutakest under the sun. Ecclesiastes 9:9

Whoso findeth a wife findeth a good thing, and obtaineth favour of the Lord. Proverbs 18:22

True love is God's gift that mirrors His love for us—passionate, committed, and sacrificial.

Preparing for Marriage

Trust in the Lord with all thine heart; and lean not unto thine own understanding. In all thy waysacknowledge him, and he shall direct thy paths. Proverbs 3:5-6

Delight thyself also in the Lord; and he shall give thee the desires of thine heart. Psalms 37:4

Be ye not unequally yoked together with unbelievers: for what fellowship hath righteousness withunrighteousness? and what communion hath light with darkness? 2 Corinthians 6:14

But seek ye first the kingdom of God, and his righteousness; and all these things shall be added unto you.Matthew 6:33

The aged women likewise, that they be in behaviour as becometh holiness, not false accusers, not givento much wine, teachers of good things; That they may teach the young women to be sober, to love their husbands, to love their children. Titus 2:3-4

Whose adorning let it not be that outward adorning of plaiting the hair, and of wearing of gold, or ofputting on of apparel; But let it be the hidden man of the heart, in that which is not corruptible, even theornament of a meek and quiet spirit, which is in the sight of God of great price. 1 Peter 3:3-4

Marriage is honourable in all, and the bed undefiled: but whoremongers and adulterers God will judge.Hebrews 13:4

House and riches are the inheritance of fathers: and a prudent wife is from the Lord. Proverbs 19:14

Preparing for marriage means becoming the woman God wants you to be, not searching for theman you think you need.

Supporting Other Women

Bear ye one another's burdens, and so fulfil the law of Christ. Galatians 6:2

Wherefore comfort yourselves together, and edify one another, even as also ye do. 1 Thessalonians 5:11

And let us consider one another to provoke unto love and to good works. Hebrews 10:24

As we have therefore opportunity, let us do good unto all men, especially unto them who are of thehousehold of faith. Galatians 6:10

Two are better than one; because they have a good reward for their labour. For if they fall, the one will liftup his fellow: but woe to him that is alone when he falleth; for he hath not another to help him up.Ecclesiastes 4:9-10

Be kindly affectioned one to another with brotherly love; in honour preferring one another. Romans 12:10

Rejoice with them that do rejoice, and weep with them that weep. Romans 12:15

We then that are strong ought to bear the infirmities of the weak, and not to please ourselves. Romans15:1

But whoso hath this world's good, and seeth his brother have need, and shutteth up his bowels ofcompassion from him, how dwelleth the love of God in him? 1 John 3:17

Supporting other women means celebrating their victories and standing with them in theirstruggles.

Encouraging Others

Wherefore comfort yourselves together, and edify one another, even as also ye do. 1 Thessalonians 5:11

Let no corrupt communication proceed out of your mouth, but that which is good to the use of edifying,that it may minister grace unto the hearers. Ephesians 4:29

But exhort one another daily, while it is called To day; lest any of you be hardened through thedeceitfulness of sin. Hebrews 3:13

And let us consider one another to provoke unto love and to good works. Hebrews 10:24

Pleasant words are as an honeycomb, sweet to the soul, and health to the bones. Proverbs 16:24

A word fitly spoken is like apples of gold in pictures of silver. Proverbs 25:11

Heaviness in the heart of man maketh it stoop: but a good word maketh it glad. Proverbs 12:25

Therefore encourage one another and build each other up, just as in fact you are doing. 1 Thessalonians 5:11

Encouragement is oxygen to the soul—breathe life into others with your words and actions.

Building Bridges

Blessed are the peacemakers: for they shall be called the children of God. Matthew 5:9

Let us therefore follow after the things which make for peace, and things wherewith one may edify another. Romans 14:19

If it be possible, as much as lieth in you, live peaceably with all men. Romans 12:18

And above all these things put on charity, which is the bond of perfectness. Colossians 3:14

A soft answer turneth away wrath: but grievous words stir up anger. Proverbs 15:1

Finally, be ye all of one mind, having compassion one of another, love as brethren, be pitiful, be courteous: Not rendering evil for evil, or railing for railing: but contrariwise blessing; knowing that ye arethereunto called, that ye should inherit a blessing. 1 Peter 3:8-9

Be ye kind one to another, tenderhearted, forgiving one another, even as God for Christ's sake hathforgiven you. Ephesians 4:32

But the wisdom that is from above is first pure, then peaceable, gentle, and easy to be intreated, full ofmercy and good fruits, without partiality, and without hypocrisy. James 3:17

Building bridges requires laying down pride and extending grace across the divide.

Hospitality

Be not forgetful to entertain strangers: for thereby some have entertained angels unawares. Hebrews 13:2

Use hospitality one to another without grudging. 1 Peter 4:9
Given to hospitality. Romans 12:13

A bishop then must be blameless, the husband of one wife, vigilant, sober, of good behaviour, given tohospitality, apt to teach.
1 Timothy 3:2

For I was an hungred, and ye gave me meat: I was thirsty, and ye gave me drink: I was a stranger, and yetook me in. Matthew 25:35

And when Jesus came to the place, he looked up, and saw him, and said unto him, Zacchaeus, makehaste, and come down; for to day I must abide at thy house. Luke 19:5

As every man hath received the gift, even so minister the same one to another, as good stewards of themanifold grace of God. 1 Peter 4:10

Distributing to the necessity of saints; given to hospitality.
Romans 12:13

She stretcheth out her hand to the poor; yea, she reacheth forth her hands to the needy. Proverbs 31:20

Hospitality is love in action—opening your heart by opening your home to others.

Serving Together

And whatsoever ye do, do it heartily, as to the Lord, and not unto men. Colossians 3:23

As we have therefore opportunity, let us do good unto all men, especially unto them who are of thehousehold of faith. Galatians 6:10

For, brethren, ye have been called unto liberty; only use not liberty for an occasion to the flesh, but bylove serve one another. Galatians 5:13

As every man hath received the gift, even so minister the same one to another, as good stewards of themanifold grace of God. 1 Peter 4:10

But Jesus called them unto him, and said, Ye know that the princes of the Gentiles exercise dominion overthem, and they that are great exercise authority upon them. But it shall not be so among you: butwhosoever will be great among you, let him be your minister; And whosoever will be chief among you, lethim be your servant: Even as the Son of man came not to be ministered unto, but to minister, and to givehis life a ransom for many. Matthew 20:25-28

And let us not be weary in well doing: for in due season we shall reap, if we faint not. Galatians 6:9

Pure religion and undefiled before God and the Father is this, To visit the fatherless and widows in theiraffliction, and to keep himself unspotted from the world. James 1:27

Serving together multiplies impact and strengthens bonds—united we accomplish more for God'skingdom.

Unity Among Women

Behold, how good and how pleasant it is for brethren to dwell together in unity! Psalms 133:1

I therefore, the prisoner of the Lord, beseech you that ye walk worthy of the vocation wherewith ye arecalled, With all lowliness and meekness, with longsuffering, forbearing one another in love; Endeavouringto keep the unity of the Spirit in the bond of peace. Ephesians 4:1-3

Finally, be ye all of one mind, having compassion one of another, love as brethren, be pitiful, becourteous. 1 Peter 3:8

Now I beseech you, brethren, by the name of our Lord Jesus Christ, that ye all speak the same thing, andthat there be no divisions among you; but that ye be perfectly joined together in the same mind and inthe same judgment. 1 Corinthians 1:10

And above all these things put on charity, which is the bond of perfectness. Colossians 3:14

Fulfil ye my joy, that ye be likeminded, having the same love, being of one accord, of one mind.Philippians 2:2

That they all may be one; as thou, Father, art in me, and I in thee, that they also may be one in us: that theworld may believe that thou hast sent me. John 17:21

Unity among women reflects the heart of God and demonstrates His love to a watching world.

Godly Communication

Let your speech be alway with grace, seasoned with salt, that ye may know how ye ought to answer everyman. Colossians 4:6

Let no corrupt communication proceed out of your mouth, but that which is good to the use of edifying,that it may minister grace unto the hearers. Ephesians 4:29

A soft answer turneth away wrath: but grievous words stir up anger. Proverbs 15:1

Pleasant words are as an honeycomb, sweet to the soul, and health to the bones. Proverbs 16:24

A word fitly spoken is like apples of gold in pictures of silver. Proverbs 25:11

She openeth her mouth with wisdom; and in her tongue is the law of kindness. Proverbs 31:26

Death and life are in the power of the tongue: and they that love it shall eat the fruit thereof. Proverbs18:21

But I say unto you, That every idle word that men shall speak, they shall give account thereof in the day ofjudgment. For by thy words thou shalt be justified, and by thy words thou shalt be condemned. Matthew12:36-37

Wherefore, my beloved brethren, let every man be swift to hear, slow to speak, slow to wrath. James 1:19

Godly communication builds up rather than tears down, speaking truth in love with grace andwisdom.

Loyalty and Faithfulness

A friend loveth at all times, and a brother is born for adversity. Proverbs 17:17

Most men will proclaim every one his own goodness: but a faithful man who can find? Proverbs 20:6

Confidence in an unfaithful man in time of trouble is like a broken tooth, and a foot out of joint. Proverbs 25:19

A faithful man shall abound with blessings: but he that maketh haste to be rich shall not be innocent. Proverbs 28:20

His lord said unto him, Well done, thou good and faithful servant: thou hast been faithful over a few things, I will make thee ruler over many things: enter thou into the joy of thy lord. Matthew 25:21

And Ruth said, Intreat me not to leave thee, or to return from following after thee: for whither thou goest, I will go; and where thou lodgest, I will lodge: thy people shall be my people, and thy God my God: Where thou diest, will I die, and there will I be buried: the Lord do so to me, and more also, if ought but death part thee and me. Ruth 1:16-17

Be ye therefore followers of God, as dear children. Ephesians 5:1

Faithfulness in relationships reflects God's faithfulness to us and builds trust that withstands every storm.

Boundaries in Relationships

Above all else, guard your heart, for everything you do flows from it. Proverbs 4:23

Be ye not unequally yoked together with unbelievers: for what fellowship hath righteousness with unrighteousness? and what communion hath light with darkness? 2 Corinthians 6:14

Iron sharpeneth iron; so a man sharpeneth the countenance of his friend. Proverbs 27:17

He that walketh with wise men shall be wise: but a companion of fools shall be destroyed. Proverbs 13:20

Enter ye in at the strait gate: for wide is the gate, and broad is the way, that leadeth to destruction, andmany there be which go in thereat: Because strait is the gate, and narrow is the way, which leadeth untolife, and few there be that find it. Matthew 7:13-14

Make no friendship with an angry man; and with a furious man thou shalt not go: Lest thou learn hisways, and get a snare to thy soul. Proverbs 22:24-25

Wherefore come out from among them, and be ye separate, saith the Lord, and touch not the uncleanthing; and I will receive you.
2 Corinthians 6:17

And have no fellowship with the unfruitful works of darkness, but rather reprove them. Ephesians 5:11

Healthy boundaries protect your heart and honor God while still showing love and grace to others.

Dealing with Difficult People

If it be possible, as much as lieth in you, live peaceably with all men. Romans 12:18

But I say unto you, Love your enemies, bless them that curse you, do good to them that hate you, andpray for them which despitefully use you, and persecute you. Matthew 5:44

A soft answer turneth away wrath: but grievous words stir up anger. Proverbs 15:1

Dearly beloved, avenge not yourselves, but rather give place unto wrath: for it is written, Vengeance ismine; I will repay, saith the Lord. Therefore if thine enemy hunger, feed him; if he thirst, give him drink: forin so doing thou shalt heap coals of fire on his head. Be not overcome of evil, but overcome evil withgood. Romans 12:19-21

The discretion of a man deferreth his anger; and it is his glory to pass over a transgression. Proverbs 19:11

Be ye kind one to another, tenderhearted, forgiving one another, even as God for Christ's sake hathforgiven you. Ephesians 4:32

He that is slow to anger is better than the mighty; and he that ruleth his spirit than he that taketh a city.Proverbs 16:32

But the wisdom that is from above is first pure, then peaceable, gentle, and easy to be intreated, full ofmercy and good fruits, without partiality, and without hypocrisy. James 3:17

Dealing with difficult people requires wisdom, patience, and relying on God's strength rather thanyour own.

Women's Ministry

And it came to pass afterward, that he went throughout every city and village, preaching and shewing theglad tidings of the kingdom of God: and the twelve were with him, And certain women, which had beenhealed of evil spirits and infirmities, Mary called Magdalene, out of whom went seven devils, And Joannathe wife of Chuza Herod's steward, and Susanna, and many others, which ministered unto him of theirsubstance. Luke 8:1-3

The aged women likewise, that they be in behaviour as becometh holiness, not false accusers, not givento much wine, teachers of good things; That they may teach the young women to be sober, to love theirhusbands, to love their children. Titus 2:3-4

And he said unto them, Go ye into all the world, and preach the gospel to every creature. Mark 16:15

For we are his workmanship, created in Christ Jesus unto good works, which God hath before ordainedthat we should walk in them. Ephesians 2:10

But ye shall receive power, after that the Holy Ghost is come upon you: and ye shall be witnesses unto meboth in Jerusalem, and in all Judaea, and in Samaria, and unto the uttermost part of the earth. Acts 1:8

As every man hath received the gift, even so minister the same one to another, as good stewards of themanifold grace of God. 1 Peter 4:10

And I intreat thee also, true yokefellow, help those women which laboured with me in the gospel, withClement also, and with other my fellowlabourers, whose names are in the book of life. Philippians 4:3 Women's ministry is God's calling for women to use their unique gifts to serve Him and minister toothers in His kingdom.

Discipleship of Women

And the things that thou hast heard of me among many witnesses, the same commit thou to faithfulmen, who shall be able to teach others also. 2 Timothy 2:2

The aged women likewise, that they be in behaviour as becometh holiness, not false accusers, not givento much wine, teachers of good things; That they may teach the young women to be sober, to love theirhusbands, to love their children. Titus 2:3-4

Iron sharpeneth iron; so a man sharpeneth the countenance of his friend. Proverbs 27:17

Go ye therefore, and teach all nations, baptizing them in the name of the Father, and of the Son, and ofthe Holy Ghost: Teaching them to observe all things whatsoever I have commanded you: and, lo, I amwith you alway, even unto the end of the world. Amen. Matthew 28:19-20

Let the word of Christ dwell in you richly in all wisdom; teaching and admonishing one another in psalmsand hymns and spiritual songs, singing with grace in your hearts to the Lord. Colossians 3:16

And he gave some, apostles; and some, prophets; and some, evangelists; and some, pastors and teachers;For the perfecting of the saints, for the work of the ministry, for the edifying of the body of Christ.Ephesians 4:11-12

Take my yoke upon you, and learn of me; for I am meek and lowly in heart: and ye shall find rest untoyour souls. Matthew 11:29

Discipleship is walking alongside another woman, helping her grow in faith and become who Godcreated her to be.

Accountability Partners

Confess your faults one to another, and pray one for another, that ye may be healed. The effectual ferventprayer of a righteous man availeth much. James 5:16

Iron sharpeneth iron; so a man sharpeneth the countenance of his friend. Proverbs 27:17

Two are better than one; because they have a good reward for their labour. For if they fall, the one will liftup his fellow: but woe to him that is alone when he falleth; for he hath not another to help him up.Ecclesiastes 4:9-10

Faithful are the wounds of a friend; but the kisses of an enemy are deceitful. Proverbs 27:6

As in water face answereth to face, so the heart of man to man. Proverbs 27:19

Brethren, if a man be overtaken in a fault, ye which are spiritual, restore such an one in the spirit ofmeekness; considering thyself, lest thou also be tempted. Bear ye one another's burdens, and so fulfil thelaw of Christ. Galatians 6:1-2

Let us hold fast the profession of our faith without wavering; (for he is faithful that promised;) And let usconsider one another to provoke unto love and to good works. Hebrews 10:23-24

But exhort one another daily, while it is called To day; lest any of you be hardened through thedeceitfulness of sin. Hebrews 3:13

Accountability partners provide the courage to grow and the support to overcome life's challengestogether.

SECTION IV: MOTHERHOOD & PARENTING

Motherhood

And God blessed them, and God said unto them, Be fruitful, and multiply, and replenish the earth, andsubdue it: and have dominion over the fish of the sea, and over the fowl of the air, and over every living thing that moveth upon the earth. Genesis 1:28

Lo, children are an heritage of the Lord: and the fruit of the womb is his reward. As arrows are in the handof a mighty man; so are children of the youth. Happy is the man that hath his quiver full of them: theyshall not be ashamed, but they shall speak with the enemies in the gate. Psalms 127:3-5

Her children arise up, and call her blessed; her husband also, and he praiseth her. Proverbs 31:28

The aged women likewise, that they be in behaviour as becometh holiness, not false accusers, not givento much wine, teachers of good things; That they may teach the young women to be sober, to love theirhusbands, to love their children. Titus 2:3-4

Train up a child in the way he should go: and when he is old, he will not depart from it. Proverbs 22:6

And these words, which I command thee this day, shall be in thine heart: And thou shalt teach themdiligently unto thy children, and shalt talk of them when thou sittest in thine house, and when thouwalkest by the way, and when thou liest down, and when thou risest up. Deuteronomy 6:6-7

Can a woman forget her sucking child, that she should not have compassion on the son of her womb?yea, they may forget, yet will I not forget thee. Isaiah 49:15

But continue thou in the things which thou hast learned and hast been assured of, knowing of whomthou hast learned them; And that from a child thou hast known the holy scriptures, which are able tomake thee wise unto salvation through faith which is in Christ Jesus.
2 Timothy 3:14-15

Notwithstanding she shall be saved in childbearing, if they continue in faith and charity and holiness withsobriety. 1 Timothy 2:15

Motherhood is a sacred calling from God—a privilege to partner with Him in shaping eternal souls.

Pregnancy and Childbirth

For thou hast possessed my reins: thou hast covered me in my mother's womb. I will praise thee; for I amfearfully and wonderfully made: marvellous are thy works; and that my soul knoweth right well. Mysubstance was not hid from thee, when I was made in secret, and curiously wrought in the lowest parts ofthe earth. Thine eyes did see my substance, yet being unperfect; and in thy book all my members werewritten, which in continuance were fashioned, when as yet there was none of them. Psalms 139:13-16

Before I formed thee in the belly I knew thee; and before thou camest forth out of the womb I sanctifiedthee, and I ordained thee a prophet unto the nations. Jeremiah 1:5

Shall I bring to the birth, and not cause to bring forth? saith the Lord: shall I cause to bring forth, and shutthe womb? saith thy God. Isaiah 66:9

And she brought forth her firstborn son, and wrapped him in swaddling clothes, and laid him in amanger; because there was no room for them in the inn. Luke 2:7

A woman when she is in travail hath sorrow, because her hour is come: but as soon as she is delivered ofthe child, she remembereth no more the anguish, for joy that a man is born into the world. John 16:21

Unto the woman he said, I will greatly multiply thy sorrow and thy conception; in sorrow thou shalt bringforth children; and thy desire shall be to thy husband, and he shall rule over thee. Genesis 3:16

And Adam knew Eve his wife; and she conceived, and bare Cain, and said, I have gotten a man from theLord. Genesis 4:1

And Hannah prayed, and said, My heart rejoiceth in the Lord, mine horn is exalted in the Lord: my mouthis enlarged over mine enemies; because I rejoice in thy salvation. 1 Samuel 2:1

God's hand is upon every pregnancy—He is actively involved in the creation of each precious life.

Raising Godly Children

Train up a child in the way he should go: and when he is old, he will not depart from it. Proverbs 22:6

And these words, which I command thee this day, shall be in thine heart: And thou shalt teach themdiligently unto thy children, and shalt talk of them when thou sittest in thine house, and when thouwalkest by the way, and when thou liest down, and when thou risest up. Deuteronomy 6:6-7

And, ye fathers, provoke not your children to wrath: but bring them up in the nurture and admonition ofthe Lord. Ephesians 6:4

The just man walketh in his integrity: his children are blessed after him. Proverbs 20:7

Children, obey your parents in the Lord: for this is right. Honour thy father and mother; which is the firstcommandment with promise; That it may be well with thee, and thou mayest live long on the earth. Ephesians 6:1-3

My son, hear the instruction of thy father, and forsake not the law of thy mother: For they shall be anornament of grace unto thy head, and chains about thy neck. Proverbs 1:8-9

Only take heed to thyself, and keep thy soul diligently, lest thou forget the things which thine eyes haveseen, and lest they depart from thy heart all the days of thy life: but teach them thy sons, and thy sons'sons. Deuteronomy 4:9

But continue thou in the things which thou hast learned and hast been assured of, knowing of whomthou hast learned them; And that from a child thou hast known the holy scriptures, which are able tomake thee wise unto salvation through faith which is in Christ Jesus.
2 Timothy 3:14-15

Raising godly children requires intentional discipleship, modeling faith, and trusting God for theoutcome.

Training Children

Train up a child in the way he should go: and when he is old, he will not depart from it. Proverbs 22:6

Correct thy son, and he shall give thee rest; yea, he shall give delight unto thy soul. Proverbs 29:17

The rod and reproof give wisdom: but a child left to himself bringeth his mother to shame. Proverbs 29:15

Withhold not correction from the child: for if thou beatest him with the rod, he shall not die. Thou shaltbeat him with the rod, and shalt deliver his soul from hell. Proverbs 23:13-14

He that spareth his rod hateth his son: but he that loveth him chasteneth him betimes. Proverbs 13:24

Chasten thy son while there is hope, and let not thy soul spare for his crying. Proverbs 19:18

Furthermore we have had fathers of our flesh which corrected us, and we gave them reverence: shall wenot much rather be in subjection unto the Father of spirits, and live? For they verily for a few dayschastened us after their own pleasure; but he for our profit, that we might be partakers of his holiness.Now no chastening for the present seemeth to be joyous, but grievous: nevertheless afterward it yieldeththe peaceable fruit of righteousness unto them which are exercised thereby. Hebrews 12:9-11

And, ye fathers, provoke not your children to wrath: but bring them up in the nurture and admonition ofthe Lord. Ephesians 6:4

Training children is an act of love that prepares them for life and shapes their character foreternity.

Mother's Love

Can a woman forget her sucking child, that she should not have compassion on the son of her womb?yea, they may forget, yet will I not forget thee. Isaiah 49:15

But Jesus said, Suffer little children, and forbid them not, to come unto me: for of such is the kingdom ofheaven. Matthew 19:14

As one whom his mother comforteth, so will I comfort you; and ye shall be comforted in Jerusalem. Isaiah66:13

But we were gentle among you, even as a nurse cherisheth her children: So being affectionately desirousof you, we were willing to have imparted unto you, not the gospel of God only, but also our own souls,because ye were dear unto us. 1 Thessalonians 2:7-8

Her children arise up, and call her blessed; her husband also, and he praiseth her. Proverbs 31:28

A mother's love reflects God's unconditional love—fierce, protective, nurturing, and everlasting.

Discipline and Correction

He that spareth his rod hateth his son: but he that loveth him chasteneth him betimes. Proverbs 13:24

Withhold not correction from the child: for if thou beatest him with the rod, he shall not die. Thou shaltbeat him with the rod, and shalt deliver his soul from hell. Proverbs 23:13-14

The rod and reproof give wisdom: but a child left to himself bringeth his mother to shame. Proverbs29:15

Correct thy son, and he shall give thee rest; yea, he shall give delight unto thy soul. Proverbs 29:17

Chasten thy son while there is hope, and let not thy soul spare for his crying. Proverbs 19:18

My son, despise not the chastening of the Lord; neither be weary of his correction: For whom the Lordloveth he correcteth; even as a father the son in whom he delighteth. Proverbs 3:11-12

And, ye fathers, provoke not your children to wrath: but bring them up in the nurture and admonition ofthe Lord. Ephesians 6:4

Now no chastening for the present seemeth to be joyous, but grievous: nevertheless afterward it yieldeththe peaceable fruit of righteousness unto them which are exercised thereby. Hebrews 12:11

For they verily for a few days chastened us after their own pleasure; but he for our profit, that we mightbe partakers of his holiness. Hebrews 12:10

Biblical discipline is motivated by love and designed to develop character, not destroy the child'sspirit.

Teaching Children God's Word

And these words, which I command thee this day, shall be in thine heart: And thou shalt teach them diligently unto thy children, and shalt talk of them when thou sittest in thine house, and when thou walkest by the way, and when thou liest down, and when thou risest up. And thou shalt bind them for a sign upon thine hand, and they shall be as frontlets between thine eyes. And thou shalt write them upon the posts of thy house, and on thy gates. Deuteronomy 6:6-9

Only take heed to thyself, and keep thy soul diligently, lest thou forget the things which thine eyes have seen, and lest they depart from thy heart all the days of thy life: but teach them thy sons, and thy sons' sons. Deuteronomy 4:9

But continue thou in the things which thou hast learned and hast been assured of, knowing of whom thou hast learned them; And that from a child thou hast known the holy scriptures, which are able to make thee wise unto salvation through faith which is in Christ Jesus. 2 Timothy 3:14-15

My son, hear the instruction of thy father, and forsake not the law of thy mother: For they shall be an ornament of grace unto thy head, and chains about thy neck. Proverbs 1:8-9

The law of his God is in his heart; none of his steps shall slide. Psalms 37:31

Thy word have I hid in mine heart, that I might not sin against thee. Psalms 119:11

And all thy children shall be taught of the Lord; and great shall be the peace of thy children. Isaiah 54:13

Teaching children God's Word plants seeds of truth that will grow and bear fruit throughout their lives.

Praying for Children

And Hannah prayed, and said, My heart rejoiceth in the Lord, mine horn is exalted in the Lord: my mouthis enlarged over mine enemies; because I rejoice in thy salvation. 1 Samuel 2:1

And she vowed a vow, and said, O Lord of hosts, if thou wilt indeed look on the affliction of thinehandmaid, and remember me, and not forget thine handmaid, but wilt give unto thine handmaid a manchild, then I will give him unto the Lord all the days of his life, and there shall no rasor come upon hishead. 1 Samuel 1:11

And it was so, when the days of their feasting were gone about, that Job sent and sanctified them, androse up early in the morning, and offered burnt offerings according to the number of them all: for Jobsaid, It may be that my sons have sinned, and cursed God in their hearts. Thus did Job continually. Job 1:5

The effectual fervent prayer of a righteous man availeth much. James 5:16

Pray without ceasing. 1 Thessalonians 5:17

Be careful for nothing; but in every thing by prayer and supplication with thanksgiving let your requestsbe made known unto God. Philippians 4:6

And this is the confidence that we have in him, that, if we ask any thing according to his will, he hearethus: And if we know that he hear us, whatsoever we ask, we know that we have the petitions that wedesired of him. 1 John 5:14-15

And all things, whatsoever ye shall ask in prayer, believing, ye shall receive. Matthew 21:22

Praying for your children is one of the most powerful gifts you can give them—covering themwith God's protection and blessing.

Single Motherhood

A father of the fatherless, and a judge of the widows, is God in his holy habitation. Psalms 68:5

Leave thy fatherless children, I will preserve them alive; and let thy widows trust in me. Jeremiah 49:11

For thy Maker is thine husband; the Lord of hosts is his name; and thy Redeemer the Holy One of Israel;The God of the whole earth shall he be called. Isaiah 54:5

And the Lord, he it is that doth go before thee; he will be with thee, he will not fail thee, neither forsakethee: fear not, neither be dismayed. Deuteronomy 31:8

But my God shall supply all your need according to his riches in glory by Christ Jesus. Philippians 4:19

Cast thy burden upon the Lord, and he shall sustain thee: he shall never suffer the righteous to be moved.Psalms 55:22

The Lord is nigh unto them that are of a broken heart; and saveth such as be of a contrite spirit. Psalms34:18

I can do all things through Christ which strengtheneth me. Philippians 4:13

For he hath not despised nor abhorred the affliction of the afflicted; neither hath he hid his face from him;but when he cried unto him, he heard. Psalms 22:24

Single mothers have God as their partner—He provides strength, wisdom, and provision for everyneed.

Stepparenting

And Ruth said, Intreat me not to leave thee, or to return from following after thee: for whither thou goest, I will go; and where thou lodgest, I will lodge: thy people shall be my people, and thy God my God. Ruth 1:16

But Jesus called them unto him, and said, Suffer little children to come unto me, and forbid them not: forof such is the kingdom of God. Luke 18:16

And above all these things put on charity, which is the bond of perfectness. Colossians 3:14

Be ye kind one to another, tenderhearted, forgiving one another, even as God for Christ's sake hathforgiven you. Ephesians 4:32

And, ye fathers, provoke not your children to wrath: but bring them up in the nurture and admonition ofthe Lord. Ephesians 6:4

Pure religion and undefiled before God and the Father is this, To visit the fatherless and widows in theiraffliction, and to keep himself unspotted from the world. James 1:27

And we know that all things work together for good to them that love God, to them who are the calledaccording to his purpose. Romans 8:28

With all lowliness and meekness, with longsuffering, forbearing one another in love. Ephesians 4:2

Love is patient, love is kind—stepparenting requires extra grace, wisdom, and time to build trustand relationships.

Grandmotherhood

The glory of young men is their strength: and the beauty of old men is the grey head. Proverbs 20:29

Children's children are the crown of old men; and the glory of children are their fathers. Proverbs 17:6

But continue thou in the things which thou hast learned and hast been assured of, knowing of whomthou hast learned them; And that from a child thou hast known the holy scriptures, which are able tomake thee wise unto salvation through faith which is in Christ Jesus. 2 Timothy 3:14-15

The aged women likewise, that they be in behaviour as becometh holiness, not false accusers, not givento much wine, teachers of good things; That they may teach the young women to be sober, to love theirhusbands, to love their children. Titus 2:3-4

When I call to remembrance the unfeigned faith that is in thee, which dwelt first in thy grandmother Lois,and thy mother Eunice; and I am persuaded that in thee also. 2 Timothy 1:5

And he took them up in his arms, put his hands upon them, and blessed them. Mark 10:16

Only take heed to thyself, and keep thy soul diligently, lest thou forget the things which thine eyes haveseen, and lest they depart from thy heart all the days of thy life: but teach them thy sons, and thy sons'sons. Deuteronomy 4:9

Grandmotherhood is a sacred privilege—passing down faith, wisdom, and love to futuregenerations.

Childlessness and Infertility

And when Rachel saw that she bare Jacob no children, Rachel envied her sister; and said unto Jacob, Giveme children, or else I die. Genesis 30:1

And God remembered Rachel, and God hearkened to her, and opened her womb. Genesis 30:22

So Hannah rose up after they had eaten in Shiloh, and after they had drunk. Now Eli the priest sat upon aseat by a post of the temple of the Lord. And she was in bitterness of soul, and prayed unto the Lord, andwept sore. 1 Samuel 1:9-10

Sing, O barren, thou that didst not bear; break forth into singing, and cry aloud, thou that didst not travailwith child: for more are the children of the desolate than the children of the married wife, saith the Lord.Isaiah 54:1

For thy Maker is thine husband; the Lord of hosts is his name; and thy Redeemer the Holy One of Israel;The God of the whole earth shall he be called. Isaiah 54:5

Trust in the Lord with all thine heart; and lean not unto thine own understanding. In all thy waysacknowledge him, and he shall direct thy paths. Proverbs 3:5-6

And we know that all things work together for good to them that love God, to them who are the calledaccording to his purpose. Romans 8:28

He maketh the barren woman to keep house, and to be a joyful mother of children. Praise ye the Lord.Psalms 113:9

Childlessness does not diminish your worth—God has unique purposes and blessings for everywoman's journey.

Adoption

Pure religion and undefiled before God and the Father is this, To visit the fatherless and widows in theiraffliction, and to keep himself unspotted from the world. James 1:27

But as many as received him, to them gave he power to become the sons of God, even to them thatbelieve on his name. John 1:12

Having predestinated us unto the adoption of children by Jesus Christ to himself, according to the goodpleasure of his will. Ephesians 1:5

For ye have not received the spirit of bondage again to fear; but ye have received the Spirit of adoption,whereby we cry, Abba, Father. Romans 8:15

And will be a Father unto you, and ye shall be my sons and daughters, saith the Lord Almighty. 2Corinthians 6:18

Defend the poor and fatherless: do justice to the afflicted and needy. Psalms 82:3

He took him up in his arms, and blessed him, and said, Lord, now lettest thou thy servant depart in peace,according to thy word. Luke 2:28-29

And Mordecai took her for his own daughter. Esther 2:7

Adoption reflects God's heart for the orphaned and mirrors how He adopts us into His family.

Protective Mother

She is not afraid of the snow for her household: for all her household are clothed with scarlet. Proverbs31:21

The angel of the Lord encampeth round about them that fear him, and delivereth them. Psalms 34:7

When the enemy shall come in like a flood, the Spirit of the Lord shall lift up a standard against him.Isaiah 59:19

No weapon that is formed against thee shall prosper; and every tongue that shall rise against thee injudgment thou shalt condemn. This is the heritage of the servants of the Lord, and their righteousness isof me, saith the Lord. Isaiah 54:17

But whoso hearkeneth unto me shall dwell safely, and shall be quiet from fear of evil. Proverbs 1:33

He that dwelleth in the secret place of the most High shall abide under the shadow of the Almighty.Psalms 91:1

A mother's protective instinct mirrors God's protective care—fierce, vigilant, and rooted in love.

Nurturing Children

But we were gentle among you, even as a nurse cherisheth her children. 1 Thessalonians 2:7

Can a woman forget her sucking child, that she should not have compassion on the son of her womb?yea, they may forget, yet will I not forget thee. Isaiah 49:15

As one whom his mother comforteth, so will I comfort you; and ye shall be comforted in Jerusalem. Isaiah66:13

And Jesus called a little child unto him, and set him in the midst of them, And said, Verily I say unto you,Except ye be converted, and become as little children, ye shall not enter into the kingdom of heaven.Matthew 18:2-3

But Jesus said, Suffer little children, and forbid them not, to come unto me: for of such is the kingdom ofheaven. Matthew 19:14

Like as a father pitieth his children, so the Lord pitieth them that fear him. Psalms 103:13

He shall feed his flock like a shepherd: he shall gather the lambs with his arm, and carry them in hisbosom, and shall gently lead those that are with young. Isaiah 40:11

But the fruit of the Spirit is love, joy, peace, longsuffering, gentleness, goodness, faith. Galatians 5:22

Nurturing children creates a safe environment where they can grow, learn, and flourish.

Mother's Wisdom

My son, hear the instruction of thy father, and forsake not the law of thy mother: For they shall be anornament of grace unto thy head, and chains about thy neck. Proverbs 1:8-9

She openeth her mouth with wisdom; and in her tongue is the law of kindness. Proverbs 31:26

The heart of the wise teacheth his mouth, and addeth learning to his lips. Proverbs 16:23

If any of you lack wisdom, let him ask of God, that giveth to all men liberally, and upbraideth not; and itshall be given him. James 1:5

The fear of the Lord is the beginning of wisdom: and the knowledge of the holy is understanding.Proverbs 9:10

Happy is the man that findeth wisdom, and the man that getteth understanding. Proverbs 3:13

Get wisdom, get understanding: forget it not; neither decline from the words of my mouth. Wisdom is theprincipal thing; therefore get wisdom: and with all thy getting get understanding. Proverbs 4:5-7

But the wisdom that is from above is first pure, then peaceable, gentle, and easy to be intreated, full ofmercy and good fruits, without partiality, and without hypocrisy. James 3:17

A mother's wisdom comes from God and is passed down through words, actions, and prayers toher children.

Sacrificial Love (Mothers)

Greater love hath no man than this, that a man lay down his life for his friends. John 15:13

Herein is love, not that we loved God, but that he loved us, and sent his Son to be the propitiation for oursins. 1 John 4:10

But Jesus called them unto him, and said, Ye know that the princes of the Gentiles exercise dominion overthem, and they that are great exercise authority upon them. But it shall not be so among you: butwhosoever will be great among you, let him be your minister; And whosoever will be chief among you, lethim be your servant: Even as the Son of man came not to be ministered unto, but to minister, and to givehis life a ransom for many. Matthew 20:25-28

For, brethren, ye have been called unto liberty; only use not liberty for an occasion to the flesh, but bylove serve one another. Galatians 5:13

And walk in love, as Christ also hath loved us, and hath given himself for us an offering and a sacrifice toGod for a sweetsmelling savour. Ephesians 5:2

Hereby perceive we the love of God, because he laid down his life for us: and we ought to lay down ourlives for the brethren. 1 John 3:16

A mother's sacrificial love reflects Christ's love—selfless, giving, and willing to pay any price forher children.

Working Mothers

She considereth a field, and buyeth it: with the fruit of her hands she planteth a vineyard. She girdeth herloins with strength, and strengtheneth her arms. She perceiveth that her merchandise is good: her candlegoeth not out by night. She maketh fine linen, and selleth it; and delivereth girdles unto the merchant.Proverbs 31:16-18, 24

And whatsoever ye do, do it heartily, as to the Lord, and not unto men. Colossians 3:23

She looketh well to the ways of her household, and eateth not the bread of idleness. Proverbs 31:27

In all labour there is profit: but the talk of the lips tendeth only to penury. Proverbs 14:23

But my God shall supply all your need according to his riches in glory by Christ Jesus. Philippians 4:19

I can do all things through Christ which strengtheneth me. Philippians 4:13

But seek ye first the kingdom of God, and his righteousness; and all these things shall be added unto you.Matthew 6:33

The aged women likewise, that they be in behaviour as becometh holiness, not false accusers, not givento much wine, teachers of good things; That they may teach the young women to be sober, to love theirhusbands, to love their children. Titus 2:3-4

Working mothers serve their families through their diligence—trusting God to help them balancework and family priorities.

Homeschooling Mothers

And these words, which I command thee this day, shall be in thine heart: And thou shalt teach themdiligently unto thy children, and shalt talk of them when thou sittest in thine house, and when thouwalkest by the way, and when thou liest down, and when thou risest up. Deuteronomy 6:6-7

Train up a child in the way he should go: and when he is old, he will not depart from it. Proverbs 22:6

But continue thou in the things which thou hast learned and hast been assured of, knowing of whomthou hast learned them; And that from a child thou hast known the holy scriptures, which are able tomake thee wise unto salvation through faith which is in Christ Jesus.
2 Timothy 3:14-15

If any of you lack wisdom, let him ask of God, that giveth to all men liberally, and upbraideth not; and itshall be given him. James 1:5

My son, hear the instruction of thy father, and forsake not the law of thy mother: For they shall be anornament of grace unto thy head, and chains about thy neck. Proverbs 1:8-9

Only take heed to thyself, and keep thy soul diligently, lest thou forget the things which thine eyes haveseen, and lest they depart from thy heart all the days of thy life: but teach them thy sons, and thy sons'sons. Deuteronomy 4:9

And, ye fathers, provoke not your children to wrath: but bring them up in the nurture and admonition ofthe Lord. Ephesians 6:4

Homeschooling mothers partner with God in the daily discipleship and education of their children.

Empty Nest Mothers

The glory of young men is their strength: and the beauty of old men is the grey head. Proverbs 20:29

Children's children are the crown of old men; and the glory of children are their fathers. Proverbs 17:6

To every thing there is a season, and a time to every purpose under the heaven. Ecclesiastes 3:1

And we know that all things work together for good to them that love God, to them who are the calledaccording to his purpose. Romans 8:28

For I know the thoughts that I think toward you, saith the Lord, thoughts of peace, and not of evil, to giveyou an expected end. Jeremiah 29:11

Being confident of this very thing, that he which hath begun a good work in you will perform it until theday of Jesus Christ. Philippians 1:6

Her children arise up, and call her blessed; her husband also, and he praiseth her. Proverbs 31:28

The aged women likewise, that they be in behaviour as becometh holiness, not false accusers, not givento much wine, teachers of good things; That they may teach the young women to be sober, to love theirhusbands, to love their children. Titus 2:3-4

Empty nest mothers enter a new season of purpose—their investment in children continues tobear fruit in new ways.

SECTION V: SPIRITUAL GROWTH

Woman's Prayer Life

And he spake a parable unto them to this end, that men ought always to pray, and not to faint. Luke 18:1

Pray without ceasing. 1 Thessalonians 5:17

Be careful for nothing; but in every thing by prayer and supplication with thanksgiving let your requestsbe made known unto God. And the peace of God, which passeth all understanding, shall keep your heartsand minds through Christ Jesus. Philippians 4:6-7

And it came to pass, that, as he was praying in a certain place, when he ceased, one of his disciples saidunto him, Lord, teach us to pray, as John also taught his disciples. And he said unto them, When ye pray,say, Our Father which art in heaven, Hallowed be thy name. Thy kingdom come. Thy will be done, as inheaven, so in earth. Give us day by day our daily bread. And forgive us our sins; for we also forgive everyone that is indebted to us. And lead us not into temptation; but deliver us from evil. Luke 11:1-4

And Hannah prayed, and said, My heart rejoiceth in the Lord, mine horn is exalted in the Lord: my mouthis enlarged over mine enemies; because I rejoice in thy salvation. 1 Samuel 2:1

The effectual fervent prayer of a righteous man availeth much. James 5:16

And this is the confidence that we have in him, that, if we ask any thing according to his will, he hearethus: And if we know that he hear us, whatsoever we ask, we know that we have the petitions that wedesired of him. 1 John 5:14-15

Call unto me, and I will answer thee, and shew thee great and mighty things, which thou knowest not.Jeremiah 33:3

And all things, whatsoever ye shall ask in prayer, believing, ye shall receive. Matthew 21:22

Prayer is a woman's lifeline to God—her source of strength, guidance, and intimate fellowship withHim.

Studying God's Word

Study to shew thyself approved unto God, a workman that needeth not to be ashamed, rightly dividingthe word of truth. 2 Timothy 2:15

Thy word have I hid in mine heart, that I might not sin against thee. Psalms 119:11

All scripture is given by inspiration of God, and is profitable for doctrine, for reproof, for correction, forinstruction in righteousness: That the man of God may be perfect, throughly furnished unto all goodworks. 2 Timothy 3:16-17

For the word of God is quick, and powerful, and sharper than any twoedged sword, piercing even to thedividing asunder of soul and spirit, and of the joints and marrow, and is a discerner of the thoughts andintents of the heart. Hebrews 4:12

So then faith cometh by hearing, and hearing by the word of God. Romans 10:17

But he answered and said, It is written, Man shall not live by bread alone, but by every word thatproceedeth out of the mouth of God. Matthew 4:4

The law of the Lord is perfect, converting the soul: the testimony of the Lord is sure, making wise thesimple. The statutes of the Lord are right, rejoicing the heart: the commandment of the Lord is pure,enlightening the eyes. Psalms 19:7-8

Search the scriptures; for in them ye think ye have eternal life: and they are they which testify of me. John5:39

These were more noble than those in Thessalonica, in that they received the word with all readiness ofmind, and searched the scriptures daily, whether those things were so. Acts 17:11

God's Word is a woman's guide for life—studying it transforms the mind and directs the path.

Worship and Praise

O come, let us worship and bow down: let us kneel before the Lord our maker. For he is our God; and weare the people of his pasture, and the sheep of his hand. Psalms 95:6-7

But the hour cometh, and now is, when the true worshippers shall worship the Father in spirit and in truth:for the Father seeketh such to worship him. God is a Spirit: and they that worship him must worship himin spirit and in truth. John 4:23-24

I will praise thee, O Lord, with my whole heart; I will shew forth all thy marvellous works. I will be glad andrejoice in thee: I will sing praise to thy name, O thou most High. Psalms 9:1-2

Let every thing that hath breath praise the Lord. Praise ye the Lord. Psalms 150:6

Enter into his gates with thanksgiving, and into his courts with praise: be thankful unto him, and bless hisname. For the Lord is good; his mercy is everlasting; and his truth endureth to all generations. Psalms100:4-5

Praise ye the Lord. Praise God in his sanctuary: praise him in the firmament of his power. Praise him for hismighty acts: praise him according to his excellent greatness. Psalms 150:1-2

Speaking to yourselves in psalms and hymns and spiritual songs, singing and making melody in yourheart to the Lord;

Giving thanks always for all things unto God and the Father in the name of our Lord Jesus Christ. Ephesians 5:19-20

By him therefore let us offer the sacrifice of praise to God continually, that is, the fruit of our lips givingthanks to his name. Hebrews 13:15

Worship and praise connect a woman's heart to God—expressing love, gratitude, and adorationfor who He is.

Fasting for Women

Howbeit this kind goeth not out but by prayer and fasting. Matthew 17:21

Is not this the fast that I have chosen? to loose the bands of wickedness, to undo the heavy burdens, andto let the oppressed go free, and that ye break every yoke? Is it not to deal thy bread to the hungry, andthat thou bring the poor that are cast out to thy house? when thou seest the naked, that thou cover him;and that thou hide not thyself from thine own flesh? Then shall thy light break forth as the morning, andthine health shall spring forth speedily: and thy righteousness shall go before thee; the glory of the Lordshall be thy rereward. Isaiah 58:6-8

Moreover when ye fast, be not, as the hypocrites, of a sad countenance: for they disfigure their faces, thatthey may appear unto men to fast. Verily I say unto you, They have their reward. But thou, when thoufastest, anoint thine head, and wash thy face; That thou appear not unto men to fast, but unto thy Fatherwhich is in secret: and thy Father, which seeth in secret, shall reward thee openly. Matthew 6:16-18

So we fasted and besought our God for this: and he was intreated of us. Ezra 8:23

And Anna, a prophetess, the daughter of Phanuel, of the tribe of Aser: she was of a great age, and hadlived with an husband seven years from her virginity; And she was a widow of about fourscore and fouryears, which departed not from the temple, but served God with fastings and prayers night and day. Luke2:36-37

Then I proclaimed a fast there, at the river of Ahava, that we might afflict ourselves before our God, toseek of him a right way for us, and for our little ones, and for all our substance. Ezra 8:21

Fasting draws women into deeper intimacy with God, creating space for spiritual breakthroughand divine encounter.

Spiritual Disciplines

But his delight is in the law of the Lord; and in his law doth he meditate day and night. Psalms 1:2

I will meditate in thy precepts, and have respect unto thy ways. I will delight myself in thy statutes: I willnot forget thy word.
Psalms 119:15-16

Study to shew thyself approved unto God, a workman that needeth not to be ashamed, rightly dividingthe word of truth. 2 Timothy 2:15

Pray without ceasing. 1 Thessalonians 5:17

But I keep under my body, and bring it into subjection: lest that by any means, when I have preached toothers, I myself should be a castaway. 1 Corinthians 9:27

I beseech you therefore, brethren, by the mercies of God, that ye present your bodies a living sacrifice,holy, acceptable unto God, which is your reasonable service. Romans 12:1

Wherefore gird up the loins of your mind, be sober, and hope to the end for the grace that is to bebrought unto you at the revelation of Jesus Christ. 1 Peter 1:13

But thou, when thou prayest, enter into thy closet, and when thou hast shut thy door, pray to thy Fatherwhich is in secret; and thy Father which seeth in secret shall reward thee openly. Matthew 6:6

Spiritual disciplines are pathways to God's presence—consistent practices that cultivate intimacyand spiritual growth.

Growing in Faith

So then faith cometh by hearing, and hearing by the word of God. Romans 10:17

But without faith it is impossible to please him: for he that cometh to God must believe that he is, andthat he is a rewarder of them that diligently seek him. Hebrews 11:6

And he said unto them, Because of your unbelief: for verily I say unto you, If ye have faith as a grain ofmustard seed, ye shall say unto this mountain, Remove hence to yonder place; and it shall remove; andnothing shall be impossible unto you. Matthew 17:20

Now faith is the substance of things hoped for, the evidence of things not seen. Hebrews 11:1

For we walk by faith, not by sight. 2 Corinthians 5:7

Looking unto Jesus the author and finisher of our faith; who for the joy that was set before him enduredthe cross, despising the shame, and is set down at the right hand of the throne of God. Hebrews 12:2

Jesus said unto him, If thou canst believe, all things are possible to him that believeth. Mark 9:23

For whatsoever is born of God overcometh the world: and this is the victory that overcometh the world,even our faith. 1 John 5:4

And Jesus answering saith unto them, Have faith in God. Mark 11:22

Faith grows through exercise—the more you trust God, the stronger your faith becomes forgreater challenges.

Overcoming Doubt

And immediately Jesus stretched forth his hand, and caught him, and said unto him, O thou of little faith,wherefore didst thou doubt? Matthew 14:31

Jesus saith unto him, Thomas, because thou hast seen me, thou hast believed: blessed are they that havenot seen, and yet have believed. John 20:29

And Jesus answering said unto them, Verily I say unto you, If ye have faith, and doubt not, ye shall notonly do this which is done to the fig tree, but also if ye shall say unto this mountain, Be thou removed,and be thou cast into the sea; it shall be done. And all things, whatsoever ye shall ask in prayer, believing,ye shall receive. Matthew 21:21-22

But let him ask in faith, nothing wavering. For he that wavereth is like a wave of the sea driven with thewind and tossed. For let not that man think that he shall receive any thing of the Lord. A double mindedman is unstable in all his ways. James 1:6-8

Now the just shall live by faith: but if any man draw back, my soul shall have no pleasure in him. But weare not of them who draw back unto perdition; but of them that believe to the saving of the soul.Hebrews 10:38-39

So then faith cometh by hearing, and hearing by the word of God. Romans 10:17

Trust in the Lord with all thine heart; and lean not unto thine own understanding. In all thy waysacknowledge him, and he shall direct thy paths. Proverbs 3:5-6

Doubt is overcome by dwelling on God's faithfulness and His proven track record in your life.

TRUSTING GOD

Trust in the Lord with all thine heart; and lean not unto thine own understanding. In all thy waysacknowledge him, and he shall direct thy paths. Proverbs 3:5-6

And they that know thy name will put their trust in thee: for thou, Lord, hast not forsaken them that seekthee. Psalms 9:10

Some trust in chariots, and some in horses: but we will remember the name of the Lord our God. Psalms20:7

It is better to trust in the Lord than to put confidence in man. It is better to trust in the Lord than to putconfidence in princes. Psalms 118:8-9

But blessed is the man that trusteth in the Lord, and whose hope the Lord is. For he shall be as a treeplanted by the waters, and that spreadeth out her roots by the river, and shall not see when heat cometh,but her leaf shall be green; and shall not be careful in the year of drought, neither shall cease fromyielding fruit. Jeremiah 17:7-8

Commit thy way unto the Lord; trust also in him; and he shall bring it to pass. Psalms 37:5

The Lord is good, a strong hold in the day of trouble; and he knoweth them that trust in him. Nahum 1:7

What time I am afraid, I will trust in thee. In God I will praise his word, in God I have put my trust; I will notfear what flesh can do unto me.
Psalms 56:3-4

Trusting God means releasing control and resting in His perfect wisdom, timing, and love.

Surrendering to God

I beseech you therefore, brethren, by the mercies of God, that ye present your bodies a living sacrifice,holy, acceptable unto God, which is your reasonable service. And be not conformed to this world: but beye transformed by the renewing of your mind, that ye may prove what is that good, and acceptable, andperfect, will of God.
Romans 12:1-2

Submit yourselves therefore to God. Resist the devil, and he will flee from you. James 4:7

Nevertheless not my will, but thine, be done. Luke 22:42

I am crucified with Christ: nevertheless I live; yet not I, but Christ liveth in me: and the life which I now livein the flesh I live by the faith of the Son of God, who loved me, and gave himself for me.
Galatians 2:20

But what things were gain to me, those I counted loss for Christ. Yea doubtless, and I count all things butloss for the excellency of the knowledge of Christ Jesus my Lord: for whom I have suffered the loss of allthings, and do count them but dung, that I may win Christ.
Philippians 3:7-8

Humble yourselves therefore under the mighty hand of God, that he may exalt you in due time: Castingall your care upon him; for he careth for you. 1 Peter 5:6-7

And he said to them all, If any man will come after me, let him deny himself, and take up his cross daily,and follow me. Luke 9:23

Surrender is not defeat—it is the pathway to victory through God's power working in and throughyou.

Walking in the Spirit

This I say then, Walk in the Spirit, and ye shall not fulfil the lust of the flesh. For the flesh lusteth againstthe Spirit, and the Spirit against the flesh: and these are contrary the one to the other: so that ye cannot do the things that ye would. But if ye be led of the Spirit, ye are not under the law. Galatians 5:16-18

But the Comforter, which is the Holy Ghost, whom the Father will send in my name, he shall teach you allthings, and bring all things to your remembrance, whatsoever I have said unto you. John 14:26

For as many as are led by the Spirit of God, they are the sons of God. Romans 8:14

If we live in the Spirit, let us also walk in the Spirit. Galatians 5:25

But ye are not in the flesh, but in the Spirit, if so be that the Spirit of God dwell in you. Now if any manhave not the Spirit of Christ, he is none of his. Romans 8:9

But when he, the Spirit of truth, is come, he will guide you into all truth: for he shall not speak of himself;but whatsoever he shall hear, that shall he speak: and he will shew you things to come. John 16:13
The Spirit itself beareth witness with our spirit, that we are the children of God. Romans 8:16

But ye shall receive power, after that the Holy Ghost is come upon you: and ye shall be witnesses unto meboth in Jerusalem, and in all Judaea, and in Samaria, and unto the uttermost part of the earth. Acts 1:8

Walking in the Spirit means yielding to His leadership and allowing Him to produce His characterthrough you.

Fruit of the Spirit

But the fruit of the Spirit is love, joy, peace, longsuffering, gentleness, goodness, faith, Meekness,temperance: against such there is no law. And they that are Christ's have crucified the flesh with theaffections and lusts. If we live in the Spirit, let us also walk in the Spirit. Galatians 5:22-25

Herein is my Father glorified, that ye bear much fruit; so shall ye be my disciples. John 15:8

I am the vine, ye are the branches: He that abideth in me, and I in him, the same bringeth forth muchfruit: for without me ye can do nothing. John 15:5

Wherefore by their fruits ye shall know them. Matthew 7:20

Being filled with the fruits of righteousness, which are by Jesus Christ, unto the glory and praise of God.Philippians 1:11

For the fruit of the Spirit is in all goodness and righteousness and truth. Ephesians 5:9

Abide in me, and I in you. As the branch cannot bear fruit of itself, except it abide in the vine; no more canye, except ye abide in me. John 15:4

Every good tree bringeth forth good fruit; but a corrupt tree bringeth forth evil fruit. Matthew 7:17

The fruit of the Spirit is evidence of God's life within—character qualities that flow naturally fromHis presence.

Spiritual Warfare for Women

For we wrestle not against flesh and blood, but against principalities, against powers, against the rulers of the darkness of this world, against spiritual wickedness in high places. Wherefore take unto you the whole armour of God, that ye may be able to withstand in the evil day, and having done all, to stand. Stand therefore, having your loins girt about with truth, and having on the breastplate of righteousness; And your feet shod with the preparation of the gospel of peace; Above all, taking the shield of faith, wherewith ye shall be able to quench all the fiery darts of the wicked. And take the helmet of salvation, and the sword of the Spirit, which is the word of God: Praying always with all prayer and supplication in the Spirit, and watching thereunto with all perseverance and supplication for all saints. Ephesians 6:12-18

Submit yourselves therefore to God. Resist the devil, and he will flee from you. James 4:7

Be sober, be vigilant; because your adversary the devil, as a roaring lion, walketh about, seeking whom he may devour: Whom resist stedfast in the faith, knowing that the same afflictions are accomplished in your brethren that are in the world. 1 Peter 5:8-9

And they overcame him by the blood of the Lamb, and by the word of their testimony; and they loved not their lives unto the death. Revelation 12:11

For though we walk in the flesh, we do not war after the flesh: (For the weapons of our warfare are not carnal, but mighty through God to the pulling down of strong holds;) Casting down imaginations, and every high thing that exalteth itself against the knowledge of God, and bringing into captivity every thought to the obedience of Christ. 2 Corinthians 10:3-5

Finally, my brethren, be strong in the Lord, and in the power of his might. Ephesians 6:10

Spiritual warfare requires women to stand firm in God's strength, wielding His truth and authority against the enemy's lies.

Intercession and Prayer

And he saw that there was no man, and wondered that there was no intercessor: therefore his arm brought salvation unto him; and his righteousness, it sustained him. Isaiah 59:16

Likewise the Spirit also helpeth our infirmities: for we know not what we should pray for as we ought: but the Spirit itself maketh intercession for us with groanings which cannot be uttered. Romans 8:26

I exhort therefore, that, first of all, supplications, prayers, intercessions, and giving of thanks, be made for all men; For kings, and for all that are in authority; that we may lead a quiet and peaceable life in all godliness and honesty. 1 Timothy 2:1-2

And he said unto them, Which of you shall have a friend, and shall go unto him at midnight, and say unto him, Friend, lend me three loaves; For a friend of mine in his journey is come to me, and I have nothing to set before him? And he from within shall answer and say, Trouble me not: the door is now shut, and my children are with me in bed; I cannot rise and give thee. I say unto you, Though he will not rise and give him, because he is his friend, yet because of his importunity he will rise and give him as many as he needeth. Luke 11:5-8

Confess your faults one to another, and pray one for another, that ye may be healed. The effectual fervent prayer of a righteous man availeth much. James 5:16

And I sought for a man among them, that should make up the hedge, and stand in the gap before me for the land, that I should not destroy it: but I found none. Ezekiel 22:30

Intercession is standing in the gap for others, partnering with God to bring His will to earth through prayer.

Hearing God's Voice

My sheep hear my voice, and I know them, and they follow me. John 10:27

And thine ears shall hear a word behind thee, saying, This is the way, walk ye in it, when ye turn to theright hand, and when ye turn to the left. Isaiah 30:21

Call unto me, and I will answer thee, and shew thee great and mighty things, which thou knowest not.Jeremiah 33:3

But when he, the Spirit of truth, is come, he will guide you into all truth: for he shall not speak of himself;but whatsoever he shall hear, that shall he speak: and he will shew you things to come. John 16:13

And after the earthquake a fire; but the Lord was not in the fire: and after the fire a still small voice. And itwas so, when Elijah heard it, that he wrapped his face in his mantle, and went out, and stood in theentering in of the cave. And, behold, there came a voice unto him, and said, What doest thou here, Elijah?1 Kings 19:12-13

The steps of a good man are ordered by the Lord: and he delighteth in his way. Psalms 37:23

And the Lord came, and stood, and called as at other times, Samuel, Samuel. Then Samuel answered,Speak; for thy servant heareth. 1 Samuel 3:10

God speaks to those who listen with expectant hearts—cultivating sensitivity to His voice throughHis Word and Spirit.

Obedience to God

If ye love me, keep my commandments. John 14:15

And Samuel said, Hath the Lord as great delight in burnt offerings and sacrifices, as in obeying the voiceof the Lord? Behold, to obey is better than sacrifice, and to hearken than the fat of rams.
1 Samuel 15:22

And hereby we do know that we know him, if we keep his commandments. He that saith, I know him, andkeepeth not his commandments, is a liar, and the truth is not in him. But whoso keepeth his word, in himverily is the love of God perfected: hereby know we that we are in him. 1 John 2:3-5

Jesus answered and said unto him, If a man love me, he will keep my words: and my Father will love him,and we will come unto him, and make our abode with him. John 14:23

But be ye doers of the word, and not hearers only, deceiving your own selves. James 1:22

And whatsoever we ask, we receive of him, because we keep his commandments, and do those thingsthat are pleasing in his sight.
1 John 3:22

Teaching them to observe all things whatsoever I have commanded you: and, lo, I am with you alway,even unto the end of the world. Amen. Matthew 28:20

And why call ye me, Lord, Lord, and do not the things which I say? Luke 6:46

Obedience is the evidence of love—it demonstrates our trust in God's wisdom and goodness.

Seeking God's Will

Trust in the Lord with all thine heart; and lean not unto thine own understanding. In all thy waysacknowledge him, and he shall direct thy paths. Proverbs 3:5-6

And be not conformed to this world: but be ye transformed by the renewing of your mind, that ye mayprove what is that good, and acceptable, and perfect, will of God. Romans 12:2

For this cause we also, since the day we heard it, do not cease to pray for you, and to desire that ye mightbe filled with the knowledge of his will in all wisdom and spiritual understanding; That ye might walkworthy of the Lord unto all pleasing, being fruitful in every good work, and increasing in the knowledgeof God. Colossians 1:9-10

Thy word is a lamp unto my feet, and a light unto my path. Psalms 119:105

The steps of a good man are ordered by the Lord: and he delighteth in his way. Psalms 37:23

Delight thyself also in the Lord; and he shall give thee the desires of thine heart. Commit thy way unto theLord; trust also in him; and he shall bring it to pass. Psalms 37:4-5

A man's heart deviseth his way: but the Lord directeth his steps. Proverbs 16:9

Nevertheless not my will, but thine, be done. Luke 22:42

Seeking God's will requires surrendering your plans and aligning your desires with His perfectpurposes.

Spiritual Maturity

Till we all come in the unity of the faith, and of the knowledge of the Son of God, unto a perfect man,unto the measure of the stature of the fulness of Christ: That we henceforth be no more children, tossedto and fro, and carried about with every wind of doctrine, by the sleight of men, and cunning craftiness,whereby they lie in wait to deceive; But speaking the truth in love, may grow up into him in all things,which is the head, even Christ. Ephesians 4:13-15

But grow in grace, and in the knowledge of our Lord and Saviour Jesus Christ. To him be glory both nowand for ever. Amen. 2 Peter 3:18

But strong meat belongeth to them that are of full age, even those who by reason of use have theirsenses exercised to discern both good and evil. Hebrews 5:14

When I was a child, I spake as a child, I understood as a child, I thought as a child: but when I became aman, I put away childish things. 1 Corinthians 13:11

As newborn babes, desire the sincere milk of the word, that ye may grow thereby. 1 Peter 2:2

And beside this, giving all diligence, add to your faith virtue; and to virtue knowledge; And to knowledgetemperance; and to temperance patience; and to patience godliness; And to godliness brotherly kindness;and to brotherly kindness charity. For if these things be in you, and abound, they make you that ye shallneither be barren nor unfruitful in the knowledge of our Lord Jesus Christ. 2 Peter 1:5-8

Spiritual maturity is measured not by years but by growth—becoming more like Christ in characterand wisdom.

Testimony and Witness

But ye shall receive power, after that the Holy Ghost is come upon you: and ye shall be witnesses unto meboth in Jerusalem, and in all Judaea, and in Samaria, and unto the uttermost part of the earth. Acts 1:8

And they overcame him by the blood of the Lamb, and by the word of their testimony; and they lovednot their lives unto the death. Revelation 12:11

But sanctify the Lord God in your hearts: and be ready always to give an answer to every man that askethyou a reason of the hope that is in you with meekness and fear. 1 Peter 3:15

Let your light so shine before men, that they may see your good works, and glorify your Father which is inheaven. Matthew 5:16

Come and hear, all ye that fear God, and I will declare what he hath done for my soul. Psalms 66:16

And many of the Samaritans of that city believed on him for the saying of the woman, which testified, Hetold me all that ever I did. John 4:39

The woman then left her waterpot, and went her way into the city, and saith to the men, Come, see aman, which told me all things that ever I did: is not this the Christ? John 4:28-29

For we cannot but speak the things which we have seen and heard. Acts 4:20

Your testimony is the story of God's work in your life—a powerful tool for pointing others toChrist.

Evangelism for Women

And he said unto them, Go ye into all the world, and preach the gospel to every creature. Mark 16:15

Go ye therefore, and teach all nations, baptizing them in the name of the Father, and of the Son, and ofthe Holy Ghost: Teaching them to observe all things whatsoever I have commanded you: and, lo, I amwith you alway, even unto the end of the world. Amen.
Matthew 28:19-20

But ye shall receive power, after that the Holy Ghost is come upon you: and ye shall be witnesses unto meboth in Jerusalem, and in all Judaea, and in Samaria, and unto the uttermost part of the earth.
 Acts 1:8

And they, when they had testified and preached the word of the Lord, returned to Jerusalem, andpreached the gospel in many villages of the Samaritans. Acts 8:25

The woman then left her waterpot, and went her way into the city, and saith to the men, Come, see aman, which told me all things that ever I did: is not this the Christ? John 4:28-29

How then shall they call on him in whom they have not believed? and how shall they believe in him ofwhom they have not heard? and how shall they hear without a preacher? Romans 10:14

For whosoever shall call upon the name of the Lord shall be saved. Romans 10:13

Let your speech be alway with grace, seasoned with salt, that ye may know how ye ought to answer everyman. Colossians 4:6

Women are called to share the gospel—using their unique relationships and influence to reachothers for Christ.

Ministry and Service

As every man hath received the gift, even so minister the same one to another, as good stewards of themanifold grace of God. If any man speak, let him speak as the oracles of God; if any man minister, let himdo it as of the ability which God giveth: that God in all things may be glorified through Jesus Christ, towhom be praise and dominion for ever and ever. Amen. 1 Peter 4:10-11

For we are his workmanship, created in Christ Jesus unto good works, which God hath before ordainedthat we should walk in them. Ephesians 2:10

And whatsoever ye do, do it heartily, as to the Lord, and not unto men. Colossians 3:23

For, brethren, ye have been called unto liberty; only use not liberty for an occasion to the flesh, but bylove serve one another. Galatians 5:13

But Jesus called them unto him, and said, Ye know that the princes of the Gentiles exercise dominion overthem, and they that are great exercise authority upon them. But it shall not be so among you: butwhosoever will be great among you, let him be your minister; And whosoever will be chief among you, lethim be your servant: Even as the Son of man came not to be ministered unto, but to minister, and to givehis life a ransom for many. Matthew 20:25-28

Pure religion and undefiled before God and the Father is this, To visit the fatherless and widows in theiraffliction, and to keep himself unspotted from the world. James 1:27

And let us not be weary in well doing: for in due season we shall reap, if we faint not. Galatians 6:9

Ministry is serving others with the gifts God has given—expressing His love through practical actsof service.

SECTION VI: EMOTIONAL & MENTAL HEALTH

Overcoming Depression

Why art thou cast down, O my soul? and why art thou disquieted in me? hope thou in God: for I shall yet praise him for the help of his countenance. Psalms 42:5

The Lord is nigh unto them that are of a broken heart; and saveth such as be of a contrite spirit. Psalms 34:18

He healeth the broken in heart, and bindeth up their wounds. Psalms 147:3

Cast thy burden upon the Lord, and he shall sustain thee: he shall never suffer the righteous to be moved. Psalms 55:22

The Spirit of the Lord God is upon me; because the Lord hath anointed me to preach good tidings unto the meek; he hath sent me to bind up the brokenhearted, to proclaim liberty to the captives, and the opening of the prison to them that are bound; To proclaim the acceptable year of the Lord, and the day of vengeance of our God; to comfort all that mourn; To appoint unto them that mourn in Zion, to give unto them beauty for ashes, the oil of joy for mourning, the garment of praise for the spirit of heaviness; that they might be called trees of righteousness, the planting of the Lord, that he might be glorified. Isaiah 61:1-3

Weeping may endure for a night, but joy cometh in the morning. Psalms 30:5

But they that wait upon the Lord shall renew their strength; they shall mount up with wings as eagles; they shall run, and not be weary; and they shall walk, and not faint. Isaiah 40:31

Come unto me, all ye that labour and are heavy laden, and I will give you rest. Matthew 11:28

Depression may cloud your vision, but God's love remains constant— He is your hope and your healing.

Dealing with Anxiety

Be careful for nothing; but in every thing by prayer and supplication with thanksgiving let your requestsbe made known unto God. And the peace of God, which passeth all understanding, shall keep your heartsand minds through Christ Jesus. Philippians 4:6-7

Casting all your care upon him; for he careth for you. 1 Peter 5:7

Therefore take no thought, saying, What shall we eat? or, What shall we drink? or, Wherewithal shall webe clothed? (For after all these things do the Gentiles seek:) for your heavenly Father knoweth that yehave need of all these things. But seek ye first the kingdom of God, and his righteousness; and all thesethings shall be added unto you. Take therefore no thought for the morrow: for the morrow shall takethought for the things of itself. Sufficient unto the day is the evil thereof. Matthew 6:31-34

For God hath not given us the spirit of fear; but of power, and of love, and of a sound mind. 2 Timothy 1:7

Peace I leave with you, my peace I give unto you: not as the world giveth, give I unto you. Let not yourheart be troubled, neither let it be afraid. John 14:27

Thou wilt keep him in perfect peace, whose mind is stayed on thee: because he trusteth in thee. Isaiah26:3

When thou liest down, thou shalt not be afraid: yea, thou shalt lie down, and thy sleep shall be sweet.Proverbs 3:24

Fear thou not; for I am with thee: be not dismayed; for I am thy God: I will strengthen thee; yea, I will helpthee; yea, I will uphold thee with the right hand of my righteousness. Isaiah 41:10

Anxiety is the thief of peace—but God's perfect love casts out fear and replaces worry with trust.

Managing Stress

Cast thy burden upon the Lord, and he shall sustain thee: he shall never suffer the righteous to be moved.Psalms 55:22

Come unto me, all ye that labour and are heavy laden, and I will give you rest. Take my yoke upon you,and learn of me; for I am meek and lowly in heart: and ye shall find rest unto your souls. For my yoke iseasy, and my burden is light. Matthew 11:28-30

But they that wait upon the Lord shall renew their strength; they shall mount up with wings as eagles;they shall run, and not be weary; and they shall walk, and not faint. Isaiah 40:31

He giveth power to the faint; and to them that have no might he increaseth strength. Isaiah 40:29

Be still, and know that I am God: I will be exalted among the heathen, I will be exalted in the earth. Psalms46:10

In quietness and in confidence shall be your strength: and ye would not. Isaiah 30:15

And he said unto me, My grace is sufficient for thee: for my strength is made perfect in weakness. Mostgladly therefore will I rather glory in my infirmities, that the power of Christ may rest upon me. 2Corinthians 12:9

Rest in the Lord, and wait patiently for him: fret not thyself because of him who prospereth in his way,because of the man who bringeth wicked devices to pass. Psalms 37:7

Stress is overcome not by avoiding pressure but by finding your strength and rest in God'spresence.

Healing from Trauma

He healeth the broken in heart, and bindeth up their wounds.
Psalms 147:3

The Lord is nigh unto them that are of a broken heart; and saveth such as be of a contrite spirit. Psalms34:18

The Spirit of the Lord God is upon me; because the Lord hath anointed me to preach good tidings untothe meek; he hath sent me to bind up the brokenhearted, to proclaim liberty to the captives, and theopening of the prison to them that are bound. Isaiah 61:1

To appoint unto them that mourn in Zion, to give unto them beauty for ashes, the oil of joy for mourning,the garment of praise for the spirit of heaviness; that they might be called trees of righteousness, theplanting of the Lord, that he might be glorified. Isaiah 61:3

And we know that all things work together for good to them that love God, to them who are the calledaccording to his purpose.
Romans 8:28

Weeping may endure for a night, but joy cometh in the morning.
Psalms 30:5

For I reckon that the sufferings of this present time are not worthy to be compared with the glory whichshall be revealed in us.
Romans 8:18

He hath not dealt with us after our sins; nor rewarded us according to our iniquities. For as the heaven ishigh above the earth, so great is his mercy toward them that fear him. As far as the east is from the west,so far hath he removed our transgressions from us. Psalms 103:10-12

Healing from trauma is a journey—God walks with you every step, bringing beauty from yourashes.

Self-Image and Confidence

I will praise thee; for I am fearfully and wonderfully made: marvellous are thy works; and that my soul knoweth right well. Psalms 139:14

For we are his workmanship, created in Christ Jesus unto good works, which God hath before ordained that we should walk in them. Ephesians 2:10

Since thou wast precious in my sight, thou hast been honourable, and I have loved thee: therefore will I give men for thee, and people for thy life. Isaiah 43:4

So God created man in his own image, in the image of God created he him; male and female created he them. Genesis 1:27

But ye are a chosen generation, a royal priesthood, an holy nation, a peculiar people; that ye should shew forth the praises of him who hath called you out of darkness into his marvellous light. 1 Peter 2:9

I can do all things through Christ which strengtheneth me. Philippians 4:13

For God hath not given us the spirit of fear; but of power, and of love, and of a sound mind. 2 Timothy 1:7

Being confident of this very thing, that he which hath begun a good work in you will perform it until the day of Jesus Christ. Philippians 1:6

True confidence comes not from self-esteem but from God-esteem—knowing who you are in Christ.

Overcoming Fear

For God hath not given us the spirit of fear; but of power, and of love, and of a sound mind. 2 Timothy 1:7

Fear thou not; for I am with thee: be not dismayed; for I am thy God: I will strengthen thee; yea, I will helpthee; yea, I will uphold thee with the right hand of my righteousness. Isaiah 41:10

There is no fear in love; but perfect love casteth out fear: because fear hath torment. He that feareth is notmade perfect in love. 1 John 4:18
The Lord is my light and my salvation; whom shall I fear? the Lord is the strength of my life; of whom shallI be afraid? Psalms 27:1

Have not I commanded thee? Be strong and of a good courage; be not afraid, neither be thou dismayed:for the Lord thy God is with thee whithersoever thou goest. Joshua 1:9

What time I am afraid, I will trust in thee. Psalms 56:3

The Lord is on my side; I will not fear: what can man do unto me? Psalms 118:6

Yea, though I walk through the valley of the shadow of death, I will fear no evil: for thou art with me; thyrod and thy staff they comfort me. Psalms 23:4

Be strong and of a good courage, fear not, nor be afraid of them: for the Lord thy God, he it is that dothgo with thee; he will not fail thee, nor forsake thee. Deuteronomy 31:6

Fear is overcome by faith—the more you know God's character, the less you fear yourcircumstances.

Finding Peace

Peace I leave with you, my peace I give unto you: not as the world giveth, give I unto you. Let not yourheart be troubled, neither let it be afraid. John 14:27

Thou wilt keep him in perfect peace, whose mind is stayed on thee: because he trusteth in thee. Isaiah26:3

And the peace of God, which passeth all understanding, shall keep your hearts and minds through ChristJesus. Philippians 4:7

Great peace have they which love thy law: and nothing shall offend them. Psalms 119:165

The Lord will give strength unto his people; the Lord will bless his people with peace. Psalms 29:11

Be still, and know that I am God: I will be exalted among the heathen, I will be exalted in the earth. Psalms46:10

These things I have spoken unto you, that in me ye might have peace. In the world ye shall havetribulation: but be of good cheer; I have overcome the world. John 16:33

Blessed are the peacemakers: for they shall be called the children of God. Matthew 5:9

Let the peace of God rule in your hearts, to the which also ye are called in one body; and be ye thankful.Colossians 3:15

True peace is not the absence of storms but the presence of God in the midst of them.

Joy in Trials

My brethren, count it all joy when ye fall into divers temptations; Knowing this, that the trying of yourfaith worketh patience. But let patience have her perfect work, that ye may be perfect and entire, wantingnothing. James 1:2-4

These things have I spoken unto you, that my joy might remain in you, and that your joy might be full.John 15:11

Weeping may endure for a night, but joy cometh in the morning. Psalms 30:5

And not only so, but we glory in tribulations also: knowing that tribulation worketh patience; Andpatience, experience; and experience, hope: And hope maketh not ashamed; because the love of God isshed abroad in our hearts by the Holy Ghost which is given unto us. Romans 5:3-5

But the fruit of the Spirit is love, joy, peace, longsuffering, gentleness, goodness, faith. Galatians 5:22

Rejoice in the Lord alway: and again I say, Rejoice. Philippians 4:4

But rejoice, inasmuch as ye are partakers of Christ's sufferings; that, when his glory shall be revealed, yemay be glad also with exceeding joy. 1 Peter 4:13

Ye have heard of the patience of Job, and have seen the end of the Lord; that the Lord is very pitiful, andof tender mercy. James 5:11

Joy in trials comes from knowing that God is working all things together for your good and Hisglory.

Hope in Difficult Times

Why art thou cast down, O my soul? and why art thou disquieted within me? hope thou in God: for I shallyet praise him, who is the health of my countenance, and my God. Psalms 42:11

For I know the thoughts that I think toward you, saith the Lord, thoughts of peace, and not of evil, to giveyou an expected end. Jeremiah 29:11

But they that wait upon the Lord shall renew their strength; they shall mount up with wings as eagles;they shall run, and not be weary; and they shall walk, and not faint. Isaiah 40:31

And hope maketh not ashamed; because the love of God is shed abroad in our hearts by the Holy Ghostwhich is given unto us. Romans 5:5

Blessed be the God and Father of our Lord Jesus Christ, which according to his abundant mercy hathbegotten us again unto a lively hope by the resurrection of Jesus Christ from the dead. 1 Peter 1:3

Now the God of hope fill you with all joy and peace in believing, that ye may abound in hope, throughthe power of the Holy Ghost. Romans 15:13

For we are saved by hope: but hope that is seen is not hope: for what a man seeth, why doth he yet hopefor? But if we hope for that we see not, then do we with patience wait for it. Romans 8:24-25

The Lord taketh pleasure in them that fear him, in those that hope in his mercy. Psalms 147:11

Hope anchors the soul in God's promises—even when circumstances seem hopeless, He is stillsovereign.

Emotional Healing

He healeth the broken in heart, and bindeth up their wounds. Psalms 147:3

The Lord is nigh unto them that are of a broken heart; and saveth such as be of a contrite spirit. Psalms34:18

And God shall wipe away all tears from their eyes; and there shall be no more death, neither sorrow, norcrying, neither shall there be any more pain: for the former things are passed away. Revelation 21:4

To appoint unto them that mourn in Zion, to give unto them beauty for ashes, the oil of joy for mourning,the garment of praise for the spirit of heaviness; that they might be called trees of righteousness, theplanting of the Lord, that he might be glorified. Isaiah 61:3

But he was wounded for our transgressions, he was bruised for our iniquities: the chastisement of ourpeace was upon him; and with his stripes we are healed. Isaiah 53:5

Weeping may endure for a night, but joy cometh in the morning. Psalms 30:5

Come unto me, all ye that labour and are heavy laden, and I will give you rest. Matthew 11:28

Surely he hath borne our griefs, and carried our sorrows: yet we did esteem him stricken, smitten of God,and afflicted. Isaiah 53:4

Emotional healing comes through God's gentle touch—He binds up wounds and restores the joyof your salvation.

Mental Strength

For God hath not given us the spirit of fear; but of power, and of love, and of a sound mind. 2 Timothy 1:7

And be not conformed to this world: but be ye transformed by the renewing of your mind, that ye mayprove what is that good, and acceptable, and perfect, will of God. Romans 12:2

Finally, brethren, whatsoever things are true, whatsoever things are honest, whatsoever things are just,whatsoever things are pure, whatsoever things are lovely, whatsoever things are of good report; if therebe any virtue, and if there be any praise, think on these things. Philippians 4:8

Casting down imaginations, and every high thing that exalteth itself against the knowledge of God, andbringing into captivity every thought to the obedience of Christ. 2 Corinthians 10:5

Thou wilt keep him in perfect peace, whose mind is stayed on thee: because he trusteth in thee. Isaiah26:3

For though we walk in the flesh, we do not war after the flesh: (For the weapons of our warfare are notcarnal, but mighty through God to the pulling down of strong holds;) 2 Corinthians 10:3-4

I can do all things through Christ which strengtheneth me. Philippians 4:13

This book of the law shall not depart out of thy mouth; but thou shalt meditate therein day and night,that thou mayest observe to do according to all that is written therein: for then thou shalt make thy wayprosperous, and then thou shalt have good success. Joshua 1:8

Mental strength comes from filling your mind with God's truth and taking every thought captiveto Christ.

Overcoming Negative Thoughts

Casting down imaginations, and every high thing that exalteth itself against the knowledge of God, andbringing into captivity every thought to the obedience of Christ. 2 Corinthians 10:5

Finally, brethren, whatsoever things are true, whatsoever things are honest, whatsoever things are just,whatsoever things are pure, whatsoever things are lovely, whatsoever things are of good report; if therebe any virtue, and if there be any praise, think on these things. Philippians 4:8

And be not conformed to this world: but be ye transformed by the renewing of your mind, that ye mayprove what is that good, and acceptable, and perfect, will of God. Romans 12:2

Set your affection on things above, not on things on the earth. Colossians 3:2

Thy word have I hid in mine heart, that I might not sin against thee. Psalms 119:11

For as he thinketh in his heart, so is he: Eat and drink, saith he to thee; but his heart is not with thee.Proverbs 23:7

Keep thy heart with all diligence; for out of it are the issues of life. Proverbs 4:23

Thou wilt keep him in perfect peace, whose mind is stayed on thee: because he trusteth in thee. Isaiah26:3

Negative thoughts are overcome by replacing lies with God's truth— what you think determineshow you feel.

Building Resilience

We are troubled on every side, yet not distressed; we are perplexed, but not in despair; Persecuted, butnot forsaken; cast down, but not destroyed. 2 Corinthians 4:8-9

And he said unto me, My grace is sufficient for thee: for my strength is made perfect in weakness. Mostgladly therefore will I rather glory in my infirmities, that the power of Christ may rest upon me. 2Corinthians 12:9

But they that wait upon the Lord shall renew their strength; they shall mount up with wings as eagles;they shall run, and not be weary; and they shall walk, and not faint. Isaiah 40:31

The righteous cry, and the Lord heareth, and delivereth them out of all their troubles. The Lord is nighunto them that are of a broken heart; and saveth such as be of a contrite spirit. Many are the afflictions ofthe righteous: but the Lord delivereth him out of them all.
Psalms 34:17-19

For which cause we faint not; but though our outward man perish, yet the inward man is renewed day byday. For our light affliction, which is but for a moment, worketh for us a far more exceeding and eternalweight of glory. 2 Corinthians 4:16-17

My brethren, count it all joy when ye fall into divers temptations; Knowing this, that the trying of yourfaith worketh patience. But let patience have her perfect work, that ye may be perfect and entire, wantingnothing. James 1:2-4

I can do all things through Christ which strengtheneth me.
 Philippians 4:13

Resilience is built through trials—each challenge overcome strengthens your faith and characterfor the next one.

Comfort in Grief

Blessed are they that mourn: for they shall be comforted. Matthew 5:4

The Lord is nigh unto them that are of a broken heart; and saveth such as be of a contrite spirit. Psalms34:18

Cast thy burden upon the Lord, and he shall sustain thee: he shall never suffer the righteous to be moved.Psalms 55:22

Weeping may endure for a night, but joy cometh in the morning. Psalms 30:5

Yea, though I walk through the valley of the shadow of death, I will fear no evil: for thou art with me; thyrod and thy staff they comfort me. Psalms 23:4

Jesus wept. John 11:35

As one whom his mother comforteth, so will I comfort you; and ye shall be comforted in Jerusalem. Isaiah66:13

Blessed be God, even the Father of our Lord Jesus Christ, the Father of mercies, and the God of allcomfort; Who comforteth us in all our tribulation, that we may be able to comfort them which are in anytrouble, by the comfort wherewith we ourselves are comforted of God. 2 Corinthians 1:3-4

And God shall wipe away all tears from their eyes; and there shall be no more death, neither sorrow, norcrying, neither shall there be any more pain: for the former things are passed away. Revelation 21:4

In grief, God draws near as the God of all comfort—He grieves with you and carries you throughyour sorrow.

Renewed Mind

And be not conformed to this world: but be ye transformed by the renewing of your mind, that ye mayprove what is that good, and acceptable, and perfect, will of God. Romans 12:2

Finally, brethren, whatsoever things are true, whatsoever things are honest, whatsoever things are just,whatsoever things are pure, whatsoever things are lovely, whatsoever things are of good report; if therebe any virtue, and if there be any praise, think on these things. Philippians 4:8

That ye put off concerning the former conversation the old man, which is corrupt according to thedeceitful lusts; And be renewed in the spirit of your mind; And that ye put on the new man, which afterGod is created in righteousness and true holiness. Ephesians 4:22-24

Let this mind be in you, which was also in Christ Jesus. Philippians 2:5

All scripture is given by inspiration of God, and is profitable for doctrine, for reproof, for correction, forinstruction in righteousness: That the man of God may be perfect, throughly furnished unto all goodworks. 2 Timothy 3:16-17

Thy word have I hid in mine heart, that I might not sin against thee. Psalms 119:11

Casting down imaginations, and every high thing that exalteth itself against the knowledge of God, andbringing into captivity every thought to the obedience of Christ. 2 Corinthians 10:5

A renewed mind comes through God's Word—transforming your thoughts to align with His truthand perspective.

SECTION VII: PRACTICAL LIVING

Time Management

To every thing there is a season, and a time to every purpose under the heaven. Ecclesiastes 3:1

So teach us to number our days, that we may apply our hearts unto wisdom. Psalms 90:12

She riseth also while it is yet night, and giveth meat to her household, and a portion to her maidens.Proverbs 31:15

Redeeming the time, because the days are evil. Ephesians 5:16

Walk in wisdom toward them that are without, redeeming the time. Colossians 4:5

She looketh well to the ways of her household, and eateth not the bread of idleness. Proverbs 31:27

And that ye study to be quiet, and to do your own business, and to work with your own hands, as wecommanded you; That ye may walk honestly toward them that are without, and that ye may have lack ofnothing. 1 Thessalonians 4:11-12

But seek ye first the kingdom of God, and his righteousness; and all these things shall be added unto you.Take therefore no thought for the morrow: for the morrow shall take thought for the things of itself. Sufficient unto the day is the evil thereof. Matthew 6:33-34

In all labour there is profit: but the talk of the lips tendeth only to penury. Proverbs 14:23

The plans of the diligent lead to profit as surely as haste leads to poverty. Proverbs 21:5

Time is God's gift to accomplish His purposes—manage it wisely by prioritizing what matters mostto Him.

Work and Career

And whatsoever ye do, do it heartily, as to the Lord, and not unto men; Knowing that of the Lord ye shallreceive the reward of the inheritance: for ye serve the Lord Christ. Colossians 3:23-24

Whether therefore ye eat, or drink, or whatsoever ye do, do all to the glory of God. 1 Corinthians 10:31

She considereth a field, and buyeth it: with the fruit of her hands she planteth a vineyard. She girdeth herloins with strength, and strengtheneth her arms. She perceiveth that her merchandise is good: her candlegoeth not out by night. She maketh fine linen, and selleth it; and delivereth girdles unto the merchant.
Proverbs 31:16-18, 24

In all labour there is profit: but the talk of the lips tendeth only to penury. Proverbs 14:23

The hand of the diligent shall bear rule: but the slothful shall be under tribute. Proverbs 12:24

Let him labour, working with his hands the thing which is good, that he may have to give to him thatneedeth. Ephesians 4:28

And that ye study to be quiet, and to do your own business, and to work with your own hands, as wecommanded you; That ye may walk honestly toward them that are without, and that ye may have lack ofnothing. 1 Thessalonians 4:11-12

For even when we were with you, this we commanded you, that if any would not work, neither should heeat. 2 Thessalonians 3:10

Work is worship when done unto the Lord—excellence in your career glorifies God and blessesothers.

Financial Stewardship

Honour the Lord with thy substance, and with the firstfruits of all thine increase: So shall thy barns be filled with plenty, and thy presses shall burst out with new wine. Proverbs 3:9-10

But my God shall supply all your need according to his riches in glory by Christ Jesus. Philippians 4:19

Bring ye all the tithes into the storehouse, that there may be meat in mine house, and prove me now herewith, saith the Lord of hosts, if I will not open you the windows of heaven, and pour you out a blessing, that there shall not be room enough to receive it. Malachi 3:10

Give, and it shall be given unto you; good measure, pressed down, and shaken together, and running over, shall men give into your bosom. For with the same measure that ye mete withal it shall be measured to you again. Luke 6:38

She considereth a field, and buyeth it: with the fruit of her hands she planteth a vineyard. Proverbs 31:16

For which of you, intending to build a tower, sitteth not down first, and counteth the cost, whether he have sufficient to finish it? Luke 14:28

The borrower is servant to the lender. Proverbs 22:7

But godliness with contentment is great gain. For we brought nothing into this world, and it is certain we can carry nothing out. And having food and raiment let us be therewith content. 1 Timothy 6:6-8

A good man leaveth an inheritance to his children's children: and the wealth of the sinner is laid up for the just. Proverbs 13:22

Financial stewardship honors God with His resources—give generously, save wisely, and spend purposefully.

Health and Wellness

What? know ye not that your body is the temple of the Holy Ghost which is in you, which ye have of God, and ye are not your own? For ye are bought with a price: therefore glorify God in your body, and in yourspirit, which are God's. 1 Corinthians 6:19-20

Beloved, I wish above all things that thou mayest prosper and be in health, even as thy soul prospereth. 3John 1:2

A merry heart doeth good like a medicine: but a broken spirit drieth the bones. Proverbs 17:22

Pleasant words are as an honeycomb, sweet to the soul, and health to the bones. Proverbs 16:24

But I keep under my body, and bring it into subjection: lest that by any means, when I have preached toothers, I myself should be a castaway. 1 Corinthians 9:27

And be not conformed to this world: but be ye transformed by the renewing of your mind, that ye mayprove what is that good, and acceptable, and perfect, will of God. Romans 12:2

She girdeth her loins with strength, and strengtheneth her arms. Proverbs 31:17

For bodily exercise profiteth little: but godliness is profitable unto all things, having promise of the lifethat now is, and of that which is to come. 1 Timothy 4:8

Your body is God's temple—care for it as a stewardship, maintaining health to serve Himeffectively.

Home Management

Every wise woman buildeth her house: but the foolish plucketh it down with her hands. Proverbs 14:1

She looketh well to the ways of her household, and eateth not the bread of idleness. Proverbs 31:27

Through wisdom is an house builded; and by understanding it is established: And by knowledge shall thechambers be filled with all precious and pleasant riches. Proverbs 24:3-4

As for me and my house, we will serve the Lord. Joshua 24:15

Better is a dinner of herbs where love is, than a stalled ox and hatred therewith. Proverbs 15:17

That they may teach the young women to be sober, to love their husbands, to love their children, To bediscreet, chaste, keepers at home, good, obedient to their own husbands, that the word of God be notblasphemed. Titus 2:4-5

Use hospitality one to another without grudging. 1 Peter 4:9

And whatsoever ye do, do it heartily, as to the Lord, and not unto men. Colossians 3:23

Be it known unto you therefore, men and brethren, that through this man is preached unto you theforgiveness of sins. Acts 13:38

Home management is ministry—creating a haven of peace, order, and love that reflects God'scharacter.

Decision Making

Trust in the Lord with all thine heart; and lean not unto thine own understanding. In all thy waysacknowledge him, and he shall direct thy paths. Proverbs 3:5-6

If any of you lack wisdom, let him ask of God, that giveth to all men liberally, and upbraideth not; and itshall be given him. But let him ask in faith, nothing wavering. For he that wavereth is like a wave of thesea driven with the wind and tossed. James 1:5-6

The steps of a good man are ordered by the Lord: and he delighteth in his way. Psalms 37:23

A man's heart deviseth his way: but the Lord directeth his steps. Proverbs 16:9

Commit thy works unto the Lord, and thy thoughts shall be established. Proverbs 16:3

Where no counsel is, the people fall: but in the multitude of counsellors there is safety. Proverbs 11:14

The simple believeth every word: but the prudent man looketh well to his going. Proverbs 14:15

For which of you, intending to build a tower, sitteth not down first, and counteth the cost, whether hehave sufficient to finish it?
Luke 14:28

Good decisions flow from seeking God's wisdom first and considering His Word as your ultimatecounselor.

Leadership for Women

Let no man despise thy youth; but be thou an example of the believers, in word, in conversation, incharity, in spirit, in faith, in purity.
1 Timothy 4:12

But Jesus called them unto him, and said, Ye know that the princes of the Gentiles exercise dominion overthem, and they that are great exercise authority upon them. But it shall not be so among you: butwhosoever will be great among you, let him be your minister; And whosoever will be chief among you, lethim be your servant.
Matthew 20:25-27

She openeth her mouth with wisdom; and in her tongue is the law of kindness. Proverbs 31:26

And Deborah, a prophetess, the wife of Lapidoth, she judged Israel at that time. Judges 4:4

Moreover thou shalt provide out of all the people able men, such as fear God, men of truth, hatingcovetousness; and place such over them, to be rulers of thousands, and rulers of hundreds, rulers offifties, and rulers of tens. Exodus 18:21

Let your light so shine before men, that they may see your good works, and glorify your Father which is inheaven. Matthew 5:16

Be ye followers of me, even as I also am of Christ. 1 Corinthians 11:1

Obey them that have the rule over you, and submit yourselves: for they watch for your souls, as they thatmust give account, that they may do it with joy, and not with grief: for that is unprofitable for you.
Hebrews 13:17

Godly leadership is servant leadership—influencing others through example, wisdom, andsacrificial service.

Speaking and Communication

Let your speech be alway with grace, seasoned with salt, that ye may know how ye ought to answer everyman. Colossians 4:6

Let no corrupt communication proceed out of your mouth, but that which is good to the use of edifying, that it may minister grace unto the hearers. Ephesians 4:29

She openeth her mouth with wisdom; and in her tongue is the law of kindness. Proverbs 31:26

A soft answer turneth away wrath: but grievous words stir up anger. Proverbs 15:1

Pleasant words are as an honeycomb, sweet to the soul, and health to the bones. Proverbs 16:24

A word fitly spoken is like apples of gold in pictures of silver. Proverbs 25:11

Death and life are in the power of the tongue: and they that love it shall eat the fruit thereof. Proverbs 18:21

Wherefore, my beloved brethren, let every man be swift to hear, slow to speak, slow to wrath. James 1:19

But I say unto you, That every idle word that men shall speak, they shall give account thereof in the day of judgment. For by thy words thou shalt be justified, and by thy words thou shalt be condemned. Matthew 12:36-37

Your words have power to build up or tear down—choose them carefully to bless others and honor God.

Setting Priorities

But seek ye first the kingdom of God, and his righteousness; and all these things shall be added unto you. Matthew 6:33

One thing have I desired of the Lord, that will I seek after; that I may dwell in the house of the Lord all the days of my life, to behold the beauty of the Lord, and to enquire in his temple. Psalms 27:4

But Martha was cumbered about much serving, and came to him, and said, Lord, dost thou not care that my sister hath left me to serve alone? bid her therefore that she help me. And Jesus answered and said unto her, Martha, Martha, thou art careful and troubled about many things: But one thing is needful: and Mary hath chosen that good part, which shall not be taken away from her. Luke 10:40-42

She looketh well to the ways of her household, and eateth not the bread of idleness. Proverbs 31:27

To every thing there is a season, and a time to every purpose under the heaven. Ecclesiastes 3:1

Where your treasure is, there will your heart be also. Matthew 6:21

And that ye study to be quiet, and to do your own business, and to work with your own hands, as we commanded you.
1 Thessalonians 4:11

So teach us to number our days, that we may apply our hearts unto wisdom. Psalms 90:12

Setting priorities requires wisdom to distinguish between the urgent and the important, choosing what matters eternally.

Goal Setting

For which of you, intending to build a tower, sitteth not down first, and counteth the cost, whether hehave sufficient to finish it? Lest haply, after he hath laid the foundation, and is not able to finish it, all thatbehold it begin to mock him, Saying, This man began to build, and was not able to finish. Luke 14:28-30

Commit thy works unto the Lord, and thy thoughts shall be established. Proverbs 16:3

The plans of the diligent lead to profit as surely as haste leads to poverty. Proverbs 21:5

A man's heart deviseth his way: but the Lord directeth his steps. Proverbs 16:9

Trust in the Lord with all thine heart; and lean not unto thine own understanding. In all thy waysacknowledge him, and he shall direct thy paths. Proverbs 3:5-6

I press toward the mark for the prize of the high calling of God in Christ Jesus. Philippians 3:14

Know ye not that they which run in a race run all, but one receiveth the prize? So run, that ye may obtain.And every man that striveth for the mastery is temperate in all things. Now they do it to obtain acorruptible crown; but we an incorruptible. 1 Corinthians 9:24-25

For I know the thoughts that I think toward you, saith the Lord, thoughts of peace, and not of evil, to giveyou an expected end. Jeremiah 29:11

Set goals that align with God's purposes—plans that honor Him and advance His kingdom throughyour life.

Organization and Planning

The plans of the diligent lead to profit as surely as haste leads to poverty. Proverbs 21:5

For which of you, intending to build a tower, sitteth not down first, and counteth the cost, whether hehave sufficient to finish it? Luke 14:28

She seeketh wool, and flax, and worketh willingly with her hands. She is like the merchants' ships; shebringeth her food from afar. She riseth also while it is yet night, and giveth meat to her household, and aportion to her maidens. Proverbs 31:13-15

Let all things be done decently and in order. 1 Corinthians 14:40

Commit thy works unto the Lord, and thy thoughts shall be established. Proverbs 16:3

And that ye study to be quiet, and to do your own business, and to work with your own hands, as wecommanded you; That ye may walk honestly toward them that are without, and that ye may have lack ofnothing. 1 Thessalonians 4:11-12

But all things must be done properly and in an orderly manner. 1 Corinthians 14:40

A place for everything, and everything in its place. Proverbs 31:27

Organization and planning honor God by stewarding His gifts of time and resources withexcellence.

CREATIVITY AND TALENTS

Every good gift and every perfect gift is from above, and cometh down from the Father of lights, withwhom is no variableness, neither shadow of turning. James 1:17

As every man hath received the gift, even so minister the same one to another, as good stewards of themanifold grace of God.
1 Peter 4:10

Now there are diversities of gifts, but the same Spirit. And there are differences of administrations, butthe same Lord. And there are diversities of operations, but it is the same God which worketh all in all. Butthe manifestation of the Spirit is given to every man to profit withal. 1 Corinthians 12:4-7

She maketh herself coverings of tapestry; her clothing is silk and purple. She maketh fine linen, andselleth it; and delivereth girdles unto the merchant. Proverbs 31:22, 24

And he hath filled him with the spirit of God, in wisdom, in understanding, and in knowledge, and in allmanner of workmanship; And to devise curious works, to work in gold, and in silver, and in brass. Exodus35:31-32

Whatsoever thy hand findeth to do, do it with thy might; for there is no work, nor device, nor knowledge,nor wisdom, in the grave, whither thou goest. Ecclesiastes 9:10

For we are his workmanship, created in Christ Jesus unto good works, which God hath before ordainedthat we should walk in them. Ephesians 2:10

God-given creativity and talents are meant to glorify Him and bless others—use them for Hiskingdom purposes.

Education and Learning

If any of you lack wisdom, let him ask of God, that giveth to all men liberally, and upbraideth not; and itshall be given him. James 1:5

The fear of the Lord is the beginning of knowledge: but fools despise wisdom and instruction. Proverbs1:7

Apply thine heart unto instruction, and thine ears to the words of knowledge. Proverbs 23:12

Study to shew thyself approved unto God, a workman that needeth not to be ashamed, rightly dividingthe word of truth. 2 Timothy 2:15

The heart of the prudent getteth knowledge; and the ear of the wise seeketh knowledge. Proverbs 18:15

An heart that seeketh knowledge; and the ear of the wise seeketh knowledge. Proverbs 18:15

Get wisdom, get understanding: forget it not; neither decline from the words of my mouth. Forsake hernot, and she shall preserve thee: love her, and she shall keep thee. Wisdom is the principal thing;therefore get wisdom: and with all thy getting get understanding.
Proverbs 4:5-7

Give instruction to a wise man, and he will be yet wiser: teach a just man, and he will increase in learning.Proverbs 9:9

Education and learning honor God when grounded in His truth—seek knowledge that draws youcloser to Him.

Technology and Modern Life

All things are lawful unto me, but all things are not expedient: all things are lawful for me, but I will not bebrought under the power of any. 1 Corinthians 6:12

Finally, brethren, whatsoever things are true, whatsoever things are honest, whatsoever things are just,whatsoever things are pure, whatsoever things are lovely, whatsoever things are of good report; if therebe any virtue, and if there be any praise, think on these things. Philippians 4:8

And be not conformed to this world: but be ye transformed by the renewing of your mind, that ye mayprove what is that good, and acceptable, and perfect, will of God. Romans 12:2

Let your moderation be known unto all men. The Lord is at hand. Philippians 4:5

Redeeming the time, because the days are evil. Ephesians 5:16

Whether therefore ye eat, or drink, or whatsoever ye do, do all to the glory of God. 1 Corinthians 10:31

For where your treasure is, there will your heart be also. Matthew 6:21

Set your affection on things above, not on things on the earth. Colossians 3:2

Use technology as a tool for God's glory—let it serve your purposes rather than mastering yourtime and attention.

BALANCE IN LIFE

To every thing there is a season, and a time to every purpose under the heaven. Ecclesiastes 3:1

But seek ye first the kingdom of God, and his righteousness; and all these things shall be added unto you. Matthew 6:33

Come unto me, all ye that labour and are heavy laden, and I will give you rest. Take my yoke upon you, and learn of me; for I am meek and lowly in heart: and ye shall find rest unto your souls. For my yoke is easy, and my burden is light. Matthew 11:28-30

But Martha was cumbered about much serving, and came to him, and said, Lord, dost thou not care that my sister hath left me to serve alone? bid her therefore that she help me. And Jesus answered and said unto her, Martha, Martha, thou art careful and troubled about many things: But one thing is needful: and Mary hath chosen that good part, which shall not be taken away from her. Luke 10:40-42

Let your moderation be known unto all men. The Lord is at hand. Philippians 4:5

But godliness with contentment is great gain. 1 Timothy 6:6

Six days shalt thou labour, and do all thy work: But the seventh day is the sabbath of the Lord thy God: in it thou shalt not do any work, thou, nor thy son, nor thy daughter, thy manservant, nor thy maidservant, nor thy cattle, nor thy stranger that is within thy gates. Exodus 20:9-10

And he said unto them, Come ye yourselves apart into a desert place, and rest a while: for there were many coming and going, and they had no leisure so much as to eat. Mark 6:31

Life balance comes from putting God first and finding rhythm between work, rest, relationships, and spiritual growth.

SECTION VIII: CHALLENGES & TRIALS

Overcoming Adversity

And we know that all things work together for good to them that love God, to them who are the calledaccording to his purpose.
Romans 8:28

Yea, though I walk through the valley of the shadow of death,
I will fear no evil: for thou art with me; thyrod and thy staff they comfort me. Psalms 23:4

These things I have spoken unto you, that in me ye might have peace. In the world ye shall havetribulation: but be of good cheer;
I have overcome the world. John 16:33

Many are the afflictions of the righteous: but the Lord delivereth him out of them all. Psalms 34:19

For I reckon that sufferings of this present time are not worthy to be compared with the glory whichshall be revealed in us. Romans 8:18

We are troubled on every side, yet not distressed; we are perplexed, but not in despair; Persecuted, butnot forsaken; cast down, but not destroyed. 2 Corinthians 4:8-9

And he said unto me, My grace is sufficient for thee: for my strength is made perfect in weakness. Therefore will glory in my infirmities, that the power of Christ may rest upon me. 2 Corinthians 12:9

My brethren, count it all joy when ye fall into divers temptations; Knowing this, that the trying of yourfaith worketh patience.
James 1:2-3

But they that wait upon the Lord shall renew their strength; they shall mount up with wings as eagles;they shall run, and not be weary; and they shall walk, and not faint. Isaiah 40:31

Adversity reveals God's strength in your weakness—every trial is an opportunity for His power tobe displayed.

Dealing with Rejection

All that the Father giveth me shall come to me; and him that cometh to me I will in no wise cast out. John 6:37

He is despised and rejected of men; a man of sorrows, and acquainted with grief: and we hid as it wereour faces from him; he was despised, and we esteemed him not. Isaiah 53:3

The stone which the builders refused is become the head stone of the corner. This is the Lord's doing; it ismarvellous in our eyes. Psalms 118:22-23

But ye are a chosen generation, a royal priesthood, an holy nation, a peculiar people; that ye should shewforth the praises of him who hath called you out of darkness into his marvellous light. 1 Peter 2:9

For he hath not despised nor abhorred the affliction of the afflicted; neither hath he hid his face from him;but when he cried unto him, he heard. Psalms 22:24

Since thou wast precious in my sight, thou hast been honourable, and I have loved thee: therefore will Igive men for thee, and people for thy life. Isaiah 43:4

Fear not; for thou shalt not be ashamed: neither be thou confounded; for thou shalt not be put to shame:for thou shalt forget the shame of thy youth, and shalt not remember the reproach of thy widowhoodany more. Isaiah 54:4

What shall we then say to these things? If God be for us, who can be against us? Romans 8:31

When people reject you, remember that God has chosen you—their rejection cannot change Hisacceptance and love.

FACING CRITICISM

Blessed are ye, when men shall revile you, and persecute you, and shall say all manner of evil against you falsely, for my sake. Rejoice, and be exceeding glad: for great is your reward in heaven: for so persecuted they the prophets which were before you.
Matthew 5:11-12

But when he was reviled, reviled not again; when he suffered, he threatened not; but committed himself to him that judgeth righteously.
1 Peter 2:23

Moreover if thy brother shall trespass against thee, go and tell him his fault between thee and him alone: if he shall hear thee, thou hast gained thy brother. Matthew 18:15

A soft answer turneth away wrath: but grievous words stir up anger. Proverbs 15:1

Let no corrupt communication proceed out of your mouth, but that which is good to the use of edifying, that it may minister grace unto the hearers. Ephesians 4:29

The discretion of a man deferreth his anger; and it is his glory to pass over a transgression. Proverbs 19:11

Give instruction to a wise man, and he will be yet wiser: teach a just man, and he will increase in learning. Proverbs 9:9

Faithful are the wounds of a friend; but the kisses of an enemy are deceitful. Proverbs 27:6

Face criticism with grace—learn from what is true, forgive what is false, and respond with love rather than defense.

Betrayal and Hurt

Yea, mine own familiar friend, in whom I trusted, which did eat of my bread, hath lifted up his heel againstme. Psalms 41:9

And Jesus said unto him, Friend, wherefore art thou come? Then came they, and laid hands on Jesus, andtook him. Matthew 26:50

But I say unto you, Love your enemies, bless them that curse you, do good to them that hate you, andpray for them which despitefully use you, and persecute you. Matthew 5:44

And be ye kind one to another, tenderhearted, forgiving one another, even as God for Christ's sake hathforgiven you. Ephesians 4:32

Dearly beloved, avenge not yourselves, but rather give place unto wrath: for it is written, Vengeance ismine; I will repay, saith the Lord. Therefore if thine enemy hunger, feed him; if he thirst, give him drink: forin so doing thou shalt heap coals of fire on his head. Be not overcome of evil, but overcome evil withgood. Romans 12:19-21

And Joseph said unto them, Fear not: for am I in the place of God? But as for you, ye thought evil againstme; but God meant it unto good, to bring to pass, as it is this day, to save much people alive. Genesis50:19-20

The Lord is nigh unto them that are of a broken heart; and saveth such as be of a contrite spirit. Psalms34:18

Betrayal cuts deep, but God can heal your wounds and even use the pain for His purposes andyour growth.

Loneliness

And the Lord God said, It is not good that the man should be alone; I will make him an help meet for him. Genesis 2:18

Let your conversation be without covetousness; and be content with such things as ye have: for he hath said, I will never leave thee, nor forsake thee. Hebrews 13:5

For he hath not despised nor abhorred the affliction of the afflicted; neither hath he hid his face from him; but when he cried unto him, he heard. Psalms 22:24

A father of the fatherless, and a judge of the widows, is God in his holy habitation. God setteth the solitary in families: he bringeth out those which are bound with chains: but the rebellious dwell in a dry land. Psalms 68:5-6

Cast thy burden upon the Lord, and he shall sustain thee: he shall never suffer the righteous to be moved. Psalms 55:22

When my father and my mother forsake me, then the Lord will take me up. Psalms 27:10

And, lo, I am with you alway, even unto the end of the world. Amen. Matthew 28:20

Turn thee unto me, and have mercy upon me; for I am desolate and afflicted. Psalms 25:16

In loneliness, remember that God is always with you—He is the friend who never leaves and the companion who always understands.

Disappointment

For my thoughts are not your thoughts, neither are your ways my ways, saith the Lord. For as the heavensare higher than the earth, so are my ways higher than your ways, and my thoughts than your thoughts.Isaiah 55:8-9

And we know that all things work together for good to them that love God, to them who are the calledaccording to his purpose.
Romans 8:28

Many are the plans in a man's heart, but it is the Lord's purpose that prevails. Proverbs 19:21

Trust in the Lord with all thine heart; and lean not unto thine own understanding. In all thy waysacknowledge him, and he shall direct thy paths. Proverbs 3:5-6

Hope deferred maketh the heart sick: but when the desire cometh, it is a tree of life. Proverbs 13:12

Why art thou cast down, O my soul? and why art thou disquieted within me? hope thou in God: for I shallyet praise him, who is the health of my countenance, and my God. Psalms 42:11

For I know the thoughts that I think toward you, saith the Lord, thoughts of peace, and not of evil, to giveyou an expected end. Jeremiah 29:11

But they that wait upon the Lord shall renew their strength; they shall mount up with wings as eagles;they shall run, and not be weary; and they shall walk, and not faint. Isaiah 40:31

Disappointment is God's redirection—trust that His plans are better than yours, even when youcan't see it.

Failure and Setbacks

For a just man falleth seven times, and riseth up again: but the wicked shall fall into mischief. Proverbs 24:16

The steps of a good man are ordered by the Lord: and he delighteth in his way. Though he fall, he shall not be utterly cast down: for the Lord upholdeth him with his hand. Psalms 37:23-24

And we know that all things work together for good to them that love God, to them who are the called according to his purpose. Romans 8:28

Being confident of this very thing, that he which hath begun a good work in you will perform it until the day of Jesus Christ. Philippians 1:6

If we confess our sins, he is faithful and just to forgive us our sins, and to cleanse us from all unrighteousness. 1 John 1:9

Brethren, I count not myself to have apprehended: but this one thing I do, forgetting those things which are behind, and reaching forth unto those things which are before, I press toward the mark for the prize of the high calling of God in Christ Jesus. Philippians 3:13-14

But he said unto me, My grace is sufficient for thee: for my strength is made perfect in weakness. Most gladly therefore will I rather glory in my infirmities, that the power of Christ may rest upon me. 2 Corinthians 12:9

Failure is not final—it's a stepping stone to growth, wisdom, and greater dependence on God's strength.

Persecution for Faith

Blessed are they which are persecuted for righteousness' sake: for theirs is the kingdom of heaven.Blessed are ye, when men shall revile you, and persecute you, and shall say all manner of evil against youfalsely, for my sake. Rejoice, and be exceeding glad: for great is your reward in heaven: for so persecutedthey the prophets which were before you. Matthew 5:10-12

If the world hate you, ye know that it hated me before it hated you. If ye were of the world, the worldwould love his own: but because ye are not of the world, but I have chosen you out of the world,therefore the world hateth you. John 15:18-19

Yea, and all that will live godly in Christ Jesus shall suffer persecution. 2 Timothy 3:12

And they departed from the presence of the council, rejoicing that they were counted worthy to suffershame for his name. Acts 5:41

But rejoice, inasmuch as ye are partakers of Christ's sufferings; that, when his glory shall be revealed, yemay be glad also with exceeding joy. If ye be reproached for the name of Christ, happy are ye; for thespirit of glory and of God resteth upon you: on their part he is evil spoken of, but on your part he isglorified. 1 Peter 4:13-14

For our light affliction, which is but for a moment, worketh for us a far more exceeding and eternal weightof glory. 2 Corinthians 4:17

Fear none of those things which thou shalt suffer: behold, the devil shall cast some of you into prison,that ye may be tried; and ye shall have tribulation ten days: be thou faithful unto death, and I will givethee a crown of life. Revelation 2:10

Persecution for faith is a badge of honor—you share in Christ's sufferings and will share in Hisglory.

HEALTH CHALLENGES

Is any sick among you? let him call for the elders of the church; and let them pray over him, anointing himwith oil in the name of the Lord: And the prayer of faith shall save the sick, and the Lord shall raise himup; and if he have committed sins, they shall be forgiven him. James 5:14-15

But he was wounded for our transgressions, he was bruised for our iniquities: the chastisement of ourpeace was upon him; and with his stripes we are healed. Isaiah 53:5

Heal me, O Lord, and I shall be healed; save me, and I shall be saved: for thou art my praise. Jeremiah17:14

And Jesus went about all Galilee, teaching in their synagogues, and preaching the gospel of the kingdom,and healing all manner of sickness and all manner of disease among the people. Matthew 4:23

Beloved, I wish above all things that thou mayest prosper and be in health, even as thy soul prospereth. 3John 1:2

And he said unto me, My grace is sufficient for thee: for my strength is made perfect in weakness. Mostgladly therefore will I rather glory in my infirmities, that the power of Christ may rest upon me. 2Corinthians 12:9

Who forgiveth all thine iniquities; who healeth all thy diseases. Psalms 103:3

For we know that if our earthly house of this tabernacle were dissolved, we have a building of God, anhouse not made with hands, eternal in the heavens. 2 Corinthians 5:1

Health challenges remind us of our dependence on God—whether He heals or sustains, His graceis sufficient.

Financial Difficulties

But my God shall supply all your need according to his riches in glory by Christ Jesus. Philippians 4:19

Therefore take no thought, saying, What shall we eat? or, What shall we drink? or, Wherewithal shall we be clothed? (For after all these things do the Gentiles seek:) for your heavenly Father knoweth that ye have need of all these things. But seek ye first the kingdom of God, and his righteousness; and all these things shall be added unto you. Matthew 6:31-33

I have been young, and now am old; yet have I not seen the righteous forsaken, nor his seed begging bread. Psalms 37:25

Give us this day our daily bread. Matthew 6:11

Not that I speak in respect of want: for I have learned, in whatsoever state I am, therewith to be content. I know both how to be abased, and I know how to abound: every where and in all things I am instructed both to be full and to be hungry, both to abound and to suffer need. I can do all things through Christ which strengtheneth me. Philippians 4:11-13

But godliness with contentment is great gain. For we brought nothing into this world, and it is certain we can carry nothing out. And having food and raiment let us be therewith content. 1 Timothy 6:6-8

The young lions do lack, and suffer hunger: but they that seek the Lord shall not want any good thing. Psalms 34:10

Financial difficulties teach dependence on God—He is your provider who knows your needs and will supply them.

Family Conflicts

A soft answer turneth away wrath: but grievous words stir up anger. Proverbs 15:1

If it be possible, as much as lieth in you, live peaceably with all men. Romans 12:18

Blessed are the peacemakers: for they shall be called the children of God. Matthew 5:9

Moreover if thy brother shall trespass against thee, go and tell him his fault between thee and him alone:if he shall hear thee, thou hast gained thy brother. Matthew 18:15

And be ye kind one to another, tenderhearted, forgiving one another, even as God for Christ's sake hathforgiven you. Ephesians 4:32

Let all bitterness, and wrath, and anger, and clamour, and evil speaking, be put away from you, with allmalice: And be ye kind one to another, tenderhearted, forgiving one another, even as God for Christ'ssake hath forgiven you. Ephesians 4:31-32

Honour thy father and thy mother: that thy days may be long upon the land which the Lord thy Godgiveth thee. Exodus 20:12

Above all these things put on charity, which is the bond of perfectness. And let the peace of God rule inyour hearts, to the which also ye are called in one body; and be ye thankful. Colossians 3:14-15

Family conflicts require extra grace—love unconditionally while setting healthy boundaries withwisdom.

Workplace Challenges

Servants, be obedient to them that are your masters according to the flesh, with fear and trembling, in singleness of your heart, as unto Christ; Not with eyeservice, as menpleasers; but as the servants of Christ, doing the will of God from the heart; With good will doing service, as to the Lord, and not to men: Knowing that whatsoever good thing any man doeth, the same shall he receive of the Lord, whether he be bond or free. Ephesians 6:5-8

And whatsoever ye do, do it heartily, as to the Lord, and not unto men; Knowing that of the Lord ye shall receive the reward of the inheritance: for ye serve the Lord Christ. Colossians 3:23-24

Let your light so shine before men, that they may see your good works, and glorify your Father which is in heaven. Matthew 5:16

But I say unto you, Love your enemies, bless them that curse you, do good to them that hate you, and pray for them which despitefully use you, and persecute you. Matthew 5:44

A soft answer turneth away wrath: but grievous words stir up anger. Proverbs 15:1

Whether therefore ye eat, or drink, or whatsoever ye do, do all to the glory of God. 1 Corinthians 10:31

And we know that all things work together for good to them that love God, to them who are the called according to his purpose. Romans 8:28

Workplace challenges are opportunities to demonstrate Christ's character and influence your environment for good.

Aging Gracefully

The hoary head is a crown of glory, if it be found in the way of righteousness. Proverbs 16:31

Cast me not off in the time of old age; forsake me not when my strength faileth. Psalms 71:9

And even to your old age I am he; and even to hoar hairs will I carry you: I have made, and I will bear;even I will carry, and will deliver you. Isaiah 46:4

The righteous shall flourish like the palm tree: he shall grow like a cedar in Lebanon. Those that beplanted in the house of the Lord shall flourish in the courts of our God. They shall still bring forth fruit inold age; they shall be fat and flourishing. Psalms 92:12-14

The glory of young men is their strength: and the beauty of old men is the grey head. Proverbs 20:29

But though our outward man perish, yet the inward man is renewed day by day. 2 Corinthians 4:16

The aged women likewise, that they be in behaviour as becometh holiness, not false accusers, not givento much wine, teachers of good things; That they may teach the young women to be sober, to love theirhusbands, to love their children. Titus 2:3-4

Favour is deceitful, and beauty is vain: but a woman that feareth the Lord, she shall be praised. Proverbs31:30

Aging gracefully means growing in wisdom and godliness while embracing each season of lifewith purpose.

Loss and Grief

Blessed are they that mourn: for they shall be comforted.
Matthew 5:4

The Lord is nigh unto them that are of a broken heart; and saveth such as be of a contrite spirit. Psalms34:18

Yea, though I walk through the valley of the shadow of death, I will fear no evil: for thou art with me; thyrod and thy staff they comfort me. Psalms 23:4

Weeping may endure for a night, but joy cometh in the morning. Psalms 30:5

As one whom his mother comforteth, so will I comfort you; and ye shall be comforted in Jerusalem. Isaiah66:13

Jesus wept. John 11:35

Blessed be God, even the Father of our Lord Jesus Christ, the Father of mercies, and the God of allcomfort; Who comforteth us in all our tribulation, that we may be able to comfort them which are in anytrouble, by the comfort wherewith we ourselves are comforted of God. 2 Corinthians 1:3-4

And God shall wipe away all tears from their eyes; and there shall be no more death, neither sorrow, norcrying, neither shall there be any more pain: for the former things are passed away. Revelation 21:4

For I am persuaded, that neither death, nor life, nor angels, nor principalities, nor powers, nor thingspresent, nor things to come, Nor height, nor depth, nor any other creature, shall be able to separate usfrom the love of God, which is in Christ Jesus our Lord.
Romans 8:38-39

Grief is love with nowhere to go—God holds your tears and will turn your mourning into dancing.

Transition and Change

To every thing there is a season, and a time to every purpose under the heaven. Ecclesiastes 3:1

Jesus Christ the same yesterday, and to day, and for ever. Hebrews 13:8

For I am the Lord, I change not; therefore ye sons of Jacob are not consumed. Malachi 3:6

Every good gift and every perfect gift is from above, and cometh down from the Father of lights, withwhom is no variableness, neither shadow of turning. James 1:17

And we know that all things work together for good to them that love God, to them who are the calledaccording to his purpose. Romans 8:28

Being confident of this very thing, that he which hath begun a good work in you will perform it until theday of Jesus Christ. Philippians 1:6

For I know the thoughts that I think toward you, saith the Lord, thoughts of peace, and not of evil, to giveyou an expected end. Jeremiah 29:11

The steps of a good man are ordered by the Lord: and he delighteth in his way. Psalms 37:23

Therefore if any man be in Christ, he is a new creature: old things are passed away; behold, all things arebecome new. 2 Corinthians 5:17

Change is inevitable, but God is unchanging—trust His constant love to guide you through everytransition.

SECTION IX: BIBLICAL WOMEN EXAMPLES

Women of Faith (Old Testament)

And Enoch walked with God: and he was not; for God took him. Genesis 5:24

By faith Abel offered unto God a more excellent sacrifice than Cain, by which he obtained witness that hewas righteous, God testifying of his gifts: and by it he being dead yet speaketh. Hebrews 11:4

By faith Sarah herself received strength to conceive seed, and was delivered of a child when she was pastage, because she judged him faithful who had promised. Hebrews 11:11

By faith Abraham, when he was tried, offered up Isaac: and he that had received the promises offered uphis only begotten son. Hebrews 11:17

By faith Moses, when he was come to years, refused to be called the son of Pharaoh's daughter; Choosingrather to suffer affliction with the people of God, than to enjoy the pleasures of sin for a season. Hebrews11:24-25

By faith the harlot Rahab perished not with them that believed not, when she had received the spies withpeace. Hebrews 11:31

And what shall I more say? for the time would fail me to tell of Gedeon, and of Barak, and of Samson, andof Jephthae; of David also, and Samuel, and of the prophets: Who through faith subdued kingdoms,wrought righteousness, obtained promises, stopped the mouths of lions. Hebrews 11:32-33

These all died in faith, not having received the promises, but having seen them afar off, and werepersuaded of them, and embraced them, and confessed that they were strangers and pilgrims on theearth. Hebrews 11:13

Old Testament women of faith paved the way—their examples teach us to trust God's promiseseven when we can't see the outcome.

Women of Faith (New Testament)

And Mary said, My soul doth magnify the Lord, And my spirit hath rejoiced in God my Saviour. For hehath regarded the low estate of his handmaiden: for, behold, from henceforth all generations shall call meblessed. For he that is mighty hath done to me great things; and holy is his name. Luke 1:46-49

And Mary said, Behold the handmaid of the Lord; be it unto me according to thy word. And the angeldeparted from her. Luke 1:38

And she coming in that instant gave thanks likewise unto the Lord, and spake of him to all them thatlooked for redemption in Jerusalem. Luke 2:38

Now it came to pass, as they went, that he entered into a certain village: and a certain woman namedMartha received him into her house. And she had a sister called Mary, which also sat at Jesus' feet, andheard his word. Luke 10:38-39

And, behold, a woman, which was diseased with an issue of blood twelve years, came behind him, andtouched the hem of his garment: For she said within herself, If I may but touch his garment, I shall bewhole. But Jesus turned him about, and when he saw her, he said, Daughter, be of good comfort; thy faithhath made thee whole. And the woman was made whole from that hour. Matthew 9:20-22

Then Jesus answered and said unto her, O woman, great is thy faith: be it unto thee even as thou wilt.And her daughter was made whole from that very hour. Matthew 15:28

And there was one Anna, a prophetess, the daughter of Phanuel, of the tribe of Aser: she was of a greatage, and had lived with an husband seven years from her virginity; And she was a widow of aboutfourscore and four years, which departed not from the temple, but served God with fastings and prayersnight and day. Luke 2:36-37

New Testament women of faith show us how to respond to God with surrender, persistence, andwholehearted devotion.

Courageous Women of the Bible

And who knoweth whether thou art come to the kingdom for such a time as this? Then Esther bade themreturn Mordecai this answer, Go, gather together all the Jews that are present in Shushan, and fast ye forme, and neither eat nor drink three days, night or day: I also and my maidens will fast likewise; and so willI go in unto the king, which is not according to the law: and if I perish, I perish. Esther 4:14-16

And Deborah, a prophetess, the wife of Lapidoth, she judged Israel at that time. And she dwelt under thepalm tree of Deborah between Ramah and Bethel in mount Ephraim: and the children of Israel came upto her for judgment. Judges 4:4-5

And Rahab the harlot took the two men, and hid them, and said thus, There came men unto me, but Iwist not whence they were: And it came to pass about the time of shutting of the gate, when it was dark, that the men went out: whither the men went I wot not: pursue after them quickly; for ye shall overtakethem. But she had brought them up to the roof of the house, and hid them with the stalks of flax, whichshe had laid in order upon the roof. Joshua 2:4-6

And Jael went out to meet Sisera, and said unto him, Turn in, my lord, turn in to me; fear not. And whenhe had turned in unto her into the tent, she covered him with a mantle. Judges 4:18

And Ruth said, Intreat me not to leave thee, or to return from following after thee: for whither thou goest,I will go; and where thou lodgest, I will lodge: thy people shall be my people, and thy God my God. Ruth1:16

Courageous biblical women faced impossible situations with faith, knowing God would use theirbravery for His purposes.

Wise Women of Scripture

She openeth her mouth with wisdom; and in her tongue is the law of kindness. Proverbs 31:26

Every wise woman buildeth her house: but the foolish plucketh it down with her hands. Proverbs 14:1

Then cried a wise woman out of the city, Hear, hear; say, I pray you, unto Joab, Come near hither, that I may speak with thee. And when he was come near unto her, the woman said, Art thou Joab? And he answered, I am he. Then she said unto him, Hear the words of thine handmaid. And he answered, I do hear. Then she spake, saying, They were wont to speak in old time, saying, They shall surely ask counsel at Abel: and so they ended the matter. 2 Samuel 20:16-18

And when the queen of Sheba heard of the fame of Solomon concerning the name of the Lord, she came to prove him with hard questions. And she came to Jerusalem with a very great train, with camels that bare spices, and very much gold, and precious stones: and when she was come to Solomon, she communed with him of all that was in her heart. 1 Kings 10:1-2

The woman then left her waterpot, and went her way into the city, and saith to the men, Come, see a man, which told me all things that ever I did: is not this the Christ? John 4:28-29

Now a certain woman named Lydia heard us. She was a seller of purple from the city of Thyatira, who worshiped God. The Lord opened her heart to heed the things spoken by Paul. Acts 16:14

Wise women of Scripture used their insight and understanding to influence situations for God's glory and others' good.

MOTHERS IN THE BIBLE

And Adam called his wife's name Eve; because she was the mother of all living. Genesis 3:20

And she conceived, and bare a son; and said, God hath given me a son. Genesis 4:25

And Hannah prayed, and said, My heart rejoiceth in the Lord, mine horn is exalted in the Lord: my mouthis enlarged over mine enemies; because I rejoice in thy salvation. 1 Samuel 2:1

And she vowed a vow, and said, O Lord of hosts, if thou wilt indeed look on the affliction of thinehandmaid, and remember me, and not forget thine handmaid, but wilt give unto thine handmaid a manchild, then I will give him unto the Lord all the days of his life, and there shall no rasor come upon hishead. 1 Samuel 1:11

And Isaac entreated the Lord for his wife, because she was barren: and the Lord was entreated of him,and Rebekah his wife conceived. Genesis 25:21

And Mary said, My soul doth magnify the Lord, And my spirit hath rejoiced in God my Saviour. Luke 1:46-47

And when eight days were accomplished for the circumcising of the child, his name was called JESUS,which was so named of the angel before he was conceived in the womb. Luke 2:21

Her children arise up, and call her blessed; her husband also, and he praiseth her. Proverbs 31:28

Biblical mothers show us the sacred calling of raising children with faith, prayer, and dedication toGod's purposes.

Leaders Among Biblical Women

And Deborah, a prophetess, the wife of Lapidoth, she judged Israel at that time. Judges 4:4

And Miriam the prophetess, the sister of Aaron, took a timbrel in her hand; and all the women went outafter her with timbrels and with dances. And Miriam answered them, Sing ye to the Lord, for he hathtriumphed gloriously; the horse and his rider hath he thrown into the sea. Exodus 15:20-21

And who knoweth whether thou art come to the kingdom for such a time as this? Esther 4:14

And Huldah the prophetess, the wife of Shallum the son of Tikvath, the son of Harhas, keeper of thewardrobe; (now she dwelt in Jerusalem in the college;) and they communed with her. 2 Kings 22:14

And there was one Anna, a prophetess, the daughter of Phanuel, of the tribe of Aser: she was of a greatage, and had lived with an husband seven years from her virginity; And she was a widow of aboutfourscore and four years, which departed not from the temple, but served God with fastings and prayersnight and day. Luke 2:36-37

And I intreat thee also, true yokefellow, help those women which laboured with me in the gospel, withClement also, and with other my fellowlabourers, whose names are in the book of life. Philippians 4:3

Biblical women leaders demonstrate that God uses women in positions of authority and influencewhen they submit to His calling.

Worshipping Women

And Miriam the prophetess, the sister of Aaron, took a timbrel in her hand; and all the women went out after her with timbrels and with dances. And Miriam answered them, Sing ye to the Lord, for he hath triumphed gloriously; the horse and his rider hath he thrown into the sea. Exodus 15:20-21

And Hannah prayed, and said, My soul doth magnify the Lord, mine horn is exalted in the Lord: my mouth is enlarged over mine enemies; because I rejoice in thy salvation. 1 Samuel 2:1

And Mary said, My soul doth magnify the Lord, And my spirit hath rejoiced in God my Saviour. For he hath regarded the low estate of his handmaiden: for, behold, from henceforth all generations shall call me blessed. For he that is mighty hath done to me great things; and holy is his name. Luke 1:46-49

Then took Mary a pound of ointment of spikenard, very costly, and anointed the feet of Jesus, and wiped his feet with her hair: and the house was filled with the odour of the ointment. John 12:3

And she coming in that instant gave thanks likewise unto the Lord, and spake of him to all them that looked for redemption in Jerusalem. Luke 2:38

Now it came to pass, as they went, that he entered into a certain village: and a certain woman named Martha received him into her house. And she had a sister called Mary, which also sat at Jesus' feet, and heard his word. Luke 10:38-39

Worshipping women demonstrate that true worship comes from the heart and expresses itself through surrender and adoration.

Serving Women

Now there was at Joppa a certain disciple named Tabitha, which by interpretation is called Dorcas: this woman was full of good works and almsdeeds which she did. Acts 9:36

And it came to pass afterward, that he went throughout every city and village, preaching and shewing the glad tidings of the kingdom of God: and the twelve were with him, And certain women, which had been healed of evil spirits and infirmities, Mary called Magdalene, out of whom went seven devils, And Joanna the wife of Chuza Herod's steward, and Susanna, and many others, which ministered unto him of their substance. Luke 8:1-3

Now a certain woman named Lydia heard us. She was a seller of purple from the city of Thyatira, who worshiped God. The Lord opened her heart to heed the things spoken by Paul. And when she and her household were baptized, she begged us, saying, If you have judged me to be faithful to the Lord, come to my house and stay. So she persuaded us. Acts 16:14-15

And she had a sister called Mary, which also sat at Jesus' feet, and heard his word. But Martha was cumbered about much serving, and came to him, and said, Lord, dost thou not care that my sister hath left me to serve alone? bid her therefore that she help me. Luke 10:39-40

I commend unto you Phebe our sister, which is a servant of the church which is at Cenchrea: That ye receive her in the Lord, as becometh saints, and that ye assist her in whatsoever business she hath need of you: for she hath been a succourer of many, and of myself also. Romans 16:1-2

Serving women use their gifts and resources to advance God's kingdom and meet the needs of others.

Faithful Women

And Ruth said, Intreat me not to leave thee, or to return from following after thee: for whither thou goest,I will go; and where thou lodgest, I will lodge: thy people shall be my people, and thy God my God:Where thou diest, will I die, and there will I be buried: the Lord do so to me, and more also, if ought butdeath part thee and me. Ruth 1:16-17

By faith Sarah herself received strength to conceive seed, and was delivered of a child when she was pastage, because she judged him faithful who had promised. Hebrews 11:11

And there was one Anna, a prophetess, the daughter of Phanuel, of the tribe of Aser: she was of a greatage, and had lived with an husband seven years from her virginity; And she was a widow of aboutfourscore and four years, which departed not from the temple, but served God with fastings and prayersnight and day. Luke 2:36-37

And, behold, a woman, which was diseased with an issue of blood twelve years, came behind him, andtouched the hem of his garment: For she said within herself, If I may but touch his garment, I shall bewhole. Matthew 9:20-21

When I call to remembrance the unfeigned faith that is in thee, which dwelt first in thy grandmother Lois,and thy mother Eunice; and I am persuaded that in thee also. 2 Timothy 1:5

Faithful women demonstrate unwavering loyalty to God and others, even through difficultcircumstances.

Transformed Women

And, behold, a woman in the city, which was a sinner, when she knew that Jesus sat at meat in thePharisee's house, brought an alabaster box of ointment, And stood at his feet behind him weeping, and began to wash his feet with tears, and did wipe them with the hairs of her head, and kissed his feet, andanointed them with the ointment.
Luke 7:37-38

Jesus saith unto her, Woman, where are those thine accusers? hath no man condemned thee? She said,No man, Lord. And Jesus said unto her, Neither do I condemn thee: go, and sin no more.
John 8:10-11

And he said to the woman, Thy faith hath saved thee; go in peace.
Luke 7:50

The woman then left her waterpot, and went her way into the city, and saith to the men, Come, see aman, which told me all things that ever I did: is not this the Christ? John 4:28-29

And Mary Magdalene and Mary the mother of Joses beheld where he was laid. Mark 15:47

Now when Jesus was risen early the first day of the week, he appeared first to Mary Magdalene, out ofwhom he had cast seven devils.
Mark 16:9

Therefore if any man be in Christ, he is a new creature: old things are passed away; behold, all things arebecome new. 2 Corinthians 5:17

Transformed women show that no past is too dark for God's redemption—He makes all thingsnew.

SECTION X: SPECIAL SEASONS & PURPOSE

Seasons of Waiting

But they that wait upon the Lord shall renew their strength; they shall mount up with wings as eagles;they shall run, and not be weary; and they shall walk, and not faint. Isaiah 40:31

Wait on the Lord: be of good courage, and he shall strengthen thine heart: wait, I say, on the Lord. Psalms27:14

And we desire that every one of you do shew the same diligence to the full assurance of hope unto theend: That ye be not slothful, but followers of them who through faith and patience inherit the promises.Hebrews 6:11-12

Rest in the Lord, and wait patiently for him: fret not thyself because of him who prospereth in his way,because of the man who bringeth wicked devices to pass. Psalms 37:7

I wait for the Lord, my soul doth wait, and in his word do I hope. My soul waiteth for the Lord more thanthey that watch for the morning: I say, more than they that watch for the morning. Psalms 130:5-6

For since the beginning of the world men have not heard, nor perceived by the ear, neither hath the eyeseen, O God, beside thee, what he hath prepared for him that waiteth for him. Isaiah 64:4

And it shall be said in that day, Lo, this is our God; we have waited for him, and he will save us: this is theLord; we have waited for him, we will be glad and rejoice in his salvation. Isaiah 25:9

For I know the thoughts that I think toward you, saith the Lord, thoughts of peace, and not of evil, to giveyou an expected end. Jeremiah 29:11

Seasons of waiting are not wasted seasons—God is preparing you and working behind the scenesfor your good.

Times of Celebration

Rejoice in the Lord alway: and again I say, Rejoice. Philippians 4:4
This is the day which the Lord hath made; we will rejoice and be glad in it. Psalms 118:24

And my spirit hath rejoiced in God my Saviour. Luke 1:47

Then our mouth was filled with laughter, and our tongue with singing: then said they among the heathen, The Lord hath done great things for them. The Lord hath done great things for us; whereof we are glad. Psalms 126:2-3

Thou hast turned for me my mourning into dancing: thou hast put off my sackcloth, and girded me withgladness. Psalms 30:11

And Sarah said, God hath made me to laugh, so that all that hear will laugh with me. Genesis 21:6

Rejoice with them that do rejoice, and weep with them that weep. Romans 12:15

A time to weep, and a time to laugh; a time to mourn, and a time to dance. Ecclesiastes 3:4

But the fruit of the Spirit is love, joy, peace, longsuffering, gentleness, goodness, faith. Galatians 5:22

Make a joyful noise unto the Lord, all ye lands. Serve the Lord with gladness: come before his presencewith singing. Psalms 100:1-2

Times of celebration are gifts from God—moments to acknowledge His goodness and share joywith others.

Woman's Ministry Calling

But ye shall receive power, after that the Holy Ghost is come upon you: and ye shall be witnesses unto meboth in Jerusalem, and in all Judaea, and in Samaria, and unto the uttermost part of the earth.
Acts 1:8

For we are his workmanship, created in Christ Jesus unto good works, which God hath before ordainedthat we should walk in them.
Ephesians 2:10

The aged women likewise, that they be in behaviour as becometh holiness, not false accusers, not givento much wine, teachers of good things; That they may teach the young women to be sober, to love theirhusbands, to love their children. Titus 2:3-4

And it shall come to pass in the last days, saith God, I will pour out of my Spirit upon all flesh: and yoursons and your daughters shall prophesy, and your young men shall see visions, and your old men shalldream dreams: And on my servants and on my handmaidens I will pour out in those days of my Spirit;and they shall prophesy.
Acts 2:17-18

Go ye therefore, and teach all nations, baptizing them in the name of the Father, and of the Son, and ofthe Holy Ghost: Teaching them to observe all things whatsoever I have commanded you: and, lo, I amwith you alway, even unto the end of the world. Amen.
Matthew 28:19-20

As every man hath received the gift, even so minister the same one to another, as good stewards of themanifold grace of God. 1 Peter 4:10
And he gave some, apostles; and some, prophets; and some, evangelists; and some, pastors and teachers;For the perfecting of the saints, for the work of the ministry, for the edifying of the body of Christ.Ephesians 4:11-12

And I intreat thee also, true yokefellow, help those women which laboured with me in the gospel, withClement also, and with other my fellowlabourers, whose names are in the book of life. Philippians 4:3

Your ministry calling is unique to you—discover how God wants to use your gifts to advance Hiskingdom.

Legacy and Inheritance

A good man leaveth an inheritance to his children's children: and the wealth of the sinner is laid up forthe just. Proverbs 13:22

The just man walketh in his integrity: his children are blessed after him. Proverbs 20:7

When I call to remembrance the unfeigned faith that is in thee, which dwelt first in thy grandmother Lois,and thy mother Eunice; and I am persuaded that in thee also. 2 Timothy 1:5

One generation shall praise thy works to another, and shall declare thy mighty acts. Psalms 145:4

Only take heed to thyself, and keep thy soul diligently, lest thou forget the things which thine eyes haveseen, and lest they depart from thy heart all the days of thy life: but teach them thy sons, and thy sons'sons. Deuteronomy 4:9

Her children arise up, and call her blessed; her husband also, and he praiseth her. Proverbs 31:28

The memory of the just is blessed: but the name of the wicked shall rot. Proverbs 10:7

Blessed be the God and Father of our Lord Jesus Christ, which according to his abundant mercy hathbegotten us again unto a lively hope by the resurrection of Jesus Christ from the dead, To an inheritanceincorruptible, and undefiled, and that fadeth not away, reserved in heaven for you. 1 Peter 1:3-4

The righteous shall inherit the land, and dwell therein for ever. Psalms 37:29

Train up a child in the way he should go: and when he is old, he will not depart from it. Proverbs 22:6

Your legacy is more than what you leave behind—it's the faith, values, and love you pass on tofuture generations.

Eternal Perspective for Women

While we look not at the things which are seen, but at the things which are not seen: for the things whichare seen are temporal; but the things which are not seen are eternal. 2 Corinthians 4:18

For our light affliction, which is but for a moment, worketh for us a far more exceeding and eternal weightof glory. 2 Corinthians 4:17

Set your affection on things above, not on things on the earth. For ye are dead, and your life is hid withChrist in God. When Christ, who is our life, shall appear, then shall ye also appear with him in glory. Colossians 3:2-4

But lay up for yourselves treasures in heaven, where neither moth nor rust doth corrupt, and wherethieves do not break through nor steal. For where your treasure is, there will your heart be also. Matthew6:20-21

And this is the promise that he hath promised us, even eternal life. 1 John 2:25

For God so loved the world, that he gave his only begotten Son, that whosoever believeth in him shouldnot perish, but have everlasting life. John 3:16

And this is life eternal, that they might know thee the only true God, and Jesus Christ, whom thou hastsent. John 17:3

For we know that if our earthly house of this tabernacle were dissolved, we have a building of God, anhouse not made with hands, eternal in the heavens. 2 Corinthians 5:1

And God shall wipe away all tears from their eyes; and there shall be no more death, neither sorrow, norcrying, neither shall there be any more pain: for the former things are passed away. Revelation 21:4

For I am persuaded, that neither death, nor life, nor angels, nor principalities, nor powers, nor thingspresent, nor things to come, Nor height, nor depth, nor any other creature, shall be able to separate us from the love of God, which is in Christ Jesus our Lord. Romans 8:38-39

Living with an eternal perspective transforms every moment—what you do for Christ and Hiskingdom lasts forever.

CONCLUSION

You have just completed a journey through God's Word specifically curated for the unique experiences,challenges, and calling of women. These 180 topics represent more than organized scripture—they areGod's love letters to you, His promises for your life, and His blueprint for your purpose.

As you close this book, remember that your story is not finished. God is still writing chapters of faith,breakthrough, and transformation in your life. The promises you've read are not just beautiful words—they are spiritual weapons, sources of comfort, and roadmaps for your future.

You are not an accident. You are not overlooked. You are not forgotten. You are fearfully and wonderfully made. You are chosen. You are beloved. You are equipped. You arecalled. You are destined for greatness in God's kingdom.

Take these truths with you into every season, every challenge, and every victory. When doubt whispers, letGod's Word speak louder. When circumstances seem impossible, remember the women who went beforeyou and trusted God anyway. When you feel inadequate, recall that God's strength is made perfect inweakness.

Your finest hour is not behind you—it's ahead of you. Your greatest testimony is not what you'veovercome—it's what you're about to conquer. Your most powerful influence is not in your past—it's in your future.

God has been preparing you for such a time as this. The world needs what you carry. Your family needsyour faith. Your generation needs your courage. His kingdom needs your yes.

Now go. Walk boldly in your calling. Step confidently into your destiny. Shine brightly as the daughter ofthe King you are.

Your breakthrough starts now.

OTHER TOPICAL BIBLES AVAILABLE:

BELIEVER'S TOPICAL BIBLE
WOMEN'S TOPICAL BIBLE
MEN'S TOPICAL BIBLE
TEEN'S TOPICAL BIBLE
PASTOR'S TOPICAL BIBLE
MARRIAGE TOPICAL BIBLE
FATHER'S TOPICAL BIBLE
MOTHER'S TOPICAL BIBLE
SENIOR'S TOPICAL BIBLE
MINISTER'S TOPICAL BIBLE

www.ingramcontent.com/pod-product-compliance
Lightning Source LLC
Chambersburg PA
CBHW050109170426
43198CB00014B/2506